KETCHUP VOCA

LEVEL 2 1

i-Scream edu

영어 공부의 핵심은 단어입니다.

케찹보카로 영어 단어 실력을 키우고, 상위 1% 어휘력을 따라잡아 보세요!

케찹보카 친구들

만화 스토리

친구들의 좌충우돌 일상이 그려진 재미있는 만화를 보며 단어 뜻을 배우고, 문장에 어떻게 활용되는지 알아볼 수 있어요!

Dennis
엉뚱하고 낙천적인 성격의 자유로운 영혼!
예측 불가에, 공부에도 관심이 없지만,
운이 좋아 뭘 해도 잘 풀린대요.

Rod
인내심이 크고 생각도 깊은, 다정다감 엄친아!
개구쟁이 쌍둥이 누나, 애완묘 루나가 있어
혼자 있는 것보단 함께 하는 것을 좋아해요.

Kiara
노래를 좋아하는 사교성의 아이콘!
솔직하고 모든 일에 적극적이지만,
금방 사랑에 빠지는 짝사랑 전문가래요.

Sally
논리적이고 긍정적인 모범생!
친구들과 장난도 많이 치지만, 호기심이 많아
관심 분야에 다양한 지식을 갖고 있어요.

Mong
친구들이 궁금한 것이 있을 때 나타나는 해결사!
너무 아는 것이 많아서 어느 별에서 왔는지
궁금하기도 해요.

어휘력이란?
문맥 속에서 의미를 알고
표현적으로 사용할 수 있는 능력을 뜻합니다.

KETCH UP

Know **E**xercise **T**hink **C**heck **H**abit

망각 제로 단어 기억하기 습관으로
기억 장기화

게임으로 즐겁게 리뷰하고 테스트로 더블 체크

만화 스토리 〉 단어 〉 문장 순으로
단어 의미를 이해하며 모국어처럼 습득

이미지 연상 쓰기 연습으로 실제 단어 활용, 적용

주제별로 초등 필수&고난도 단어 학습하며
상위 1% 단어 마스터

KETCHUP
makes you Catch up.

Let's catch up with KETCHUP VOCA!

How to Use

체계적인 4 Steps 시스템으로 학습 완성!

	Step 1	Step 2	Step 3	Step 4
Day 1~4	●	●	●	
Day 5	●	●	●	●

Step 1

Warm up 망각 제로 & 스토리 단어 이해로 학습 준비하기

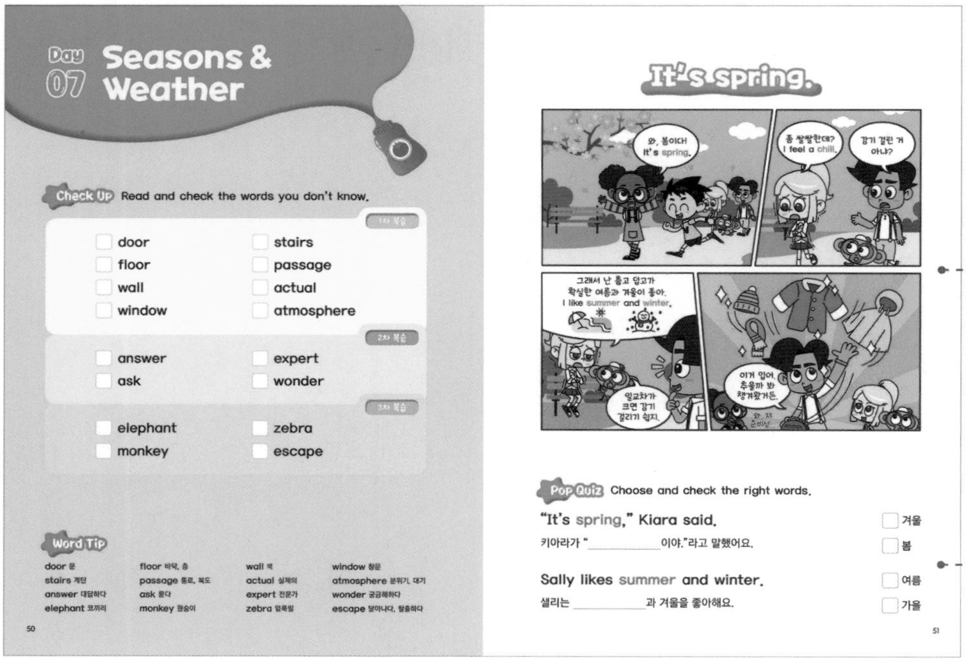

만화를 보며 단어 뜻 이해하기

문장에 적용하여 단어 뜻 찾기

※ 망각 제로는 p10에서 확인하세요!

Step 2

Catch up 듣고, 말하고, 읽고, 쓰며, 상위 1% 단어 따라잡기

QR 찍어 단어 듣고 따라 말하기 ▶ 케찹병을 색칠하며 3번 반복하기

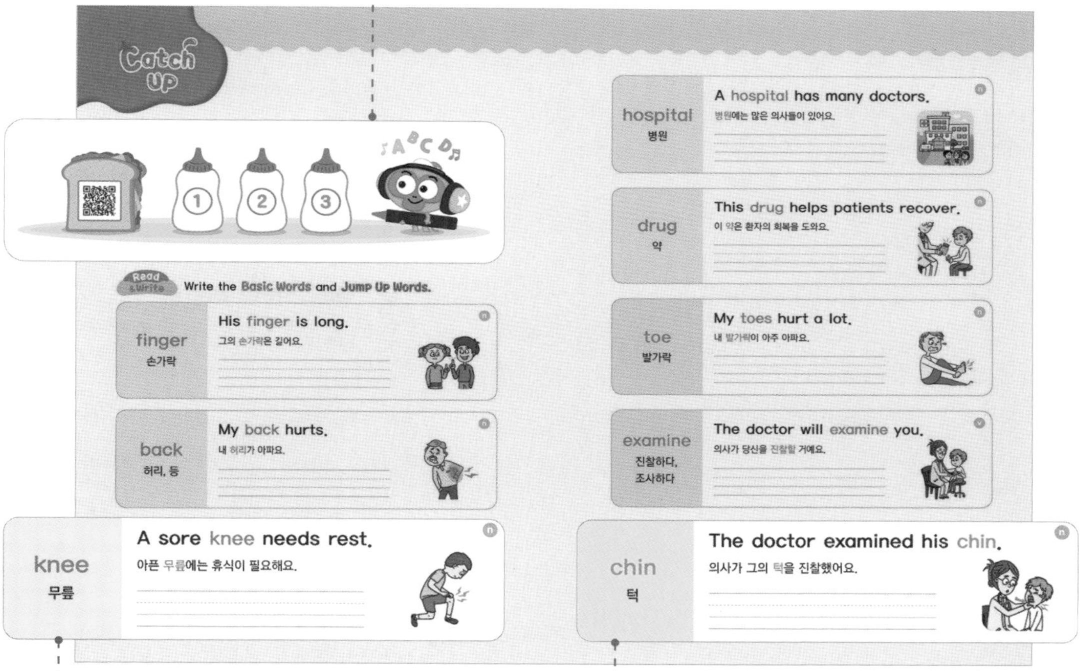

Basic Words 초등 필수 단어

Jump Up Words 고난도 단어

품사 기호

v	verb (동사)	adv	adverb (부사)	conj	conjunction (접속사)
n	noun (명사)	prep	preposition (전치사)	pron	pronoun (대명사)
a	adjective (형용사)	det	determiner (한정사)	num	numeral (수사)

케찹보카와 함께
상위 1% CATCH UP!

Step 3

Skill up 두뇌 자극 이미지 연상 학습으로 실력 강화하기

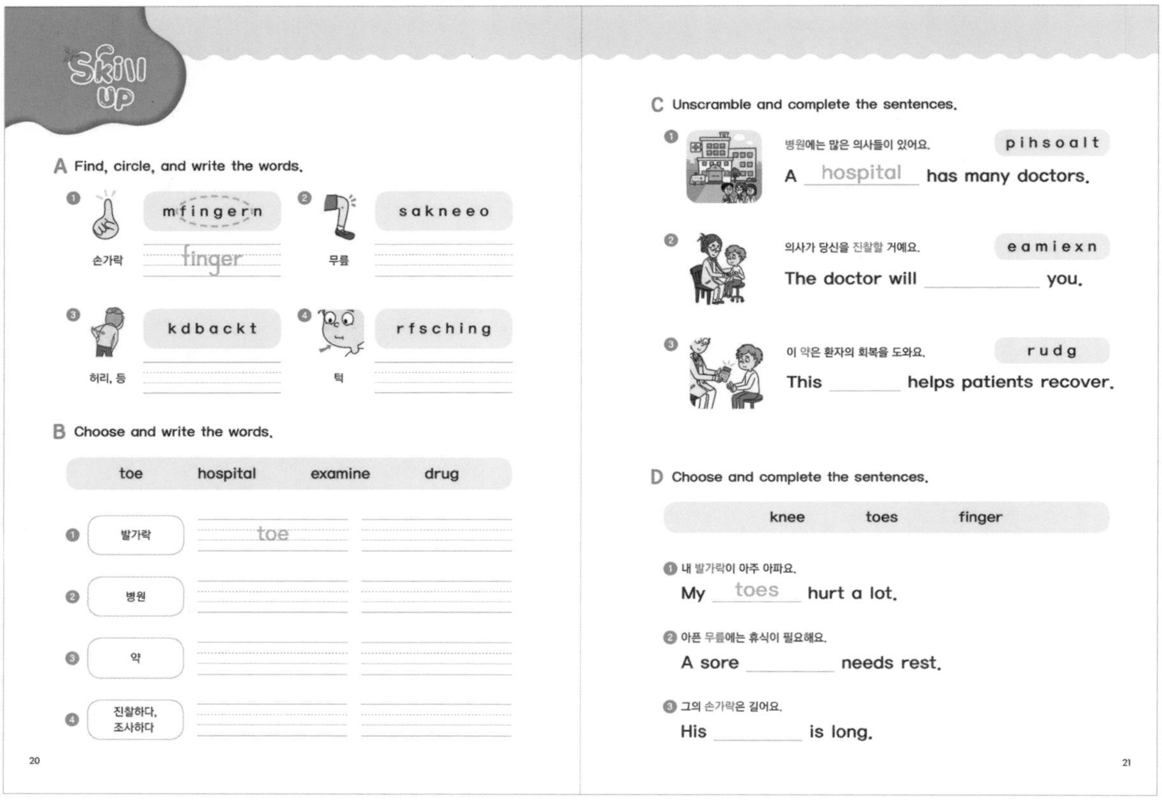

Skill up

A Find, circle, and write the words.

1. m f i n g e r n — 손가락 — finger
2. s a k n e e o — 무릎
3. k d b a c k t — 허리, 등
4. r f s c h i n g — 턱

B Choose and write the words.

toe hospital examine drug

1. 발가락 — toe
2. 병원
3. 약
4. 진찰하다, 조사하다

20

C Unscramble and complete the sentences.

1. 병원에는 많은 의사들이 있어요. p i h s o a l t
A hospital has many doctors.
2. 의사가 당신을 진찰할 거예요. e a m i e x n
The doctor will ________ you.
3. 이 약은 환자의 회복을 도와요. r u d g
This ________ helps patients recover.

D Choose and complete the sentences.

knee toes finger

1. 내 발가락이 아주 아파요.
My toes hurt a lot.
2. 아픈 무릎에는 휴식이 필요해요.
A sore ________ needs rest.
3. 그의 손가락은 길어요.
His ________ is long.

21

유형 1	유형 2	유형 3	유형 4
이미지 연상을 통해 단어 완성하기	우리말에 맞춰 스펠링 배열하여 단어 쓰기	이미지와 문장을 연결하여 단어 뜻 이해하기	배운 단어 적용하여 문장 완성하여 쓰기

Step 4

Wrap up 게임과 최종 평가를 통해 단어 학습 마무리하기

쉬어가기

다양한 유형의 재미있는 게임하며 단어 복습하기!

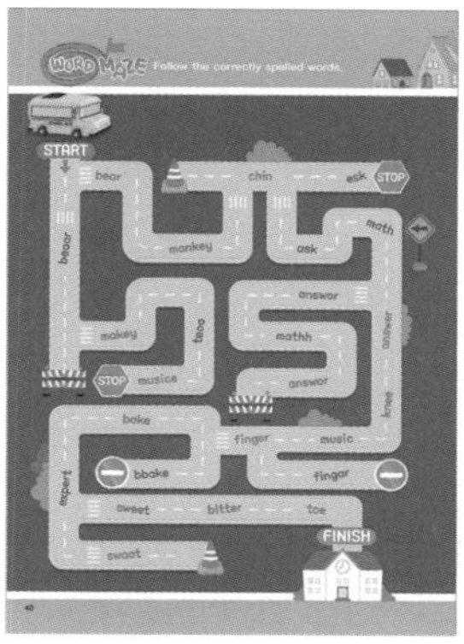

Word Maze

알맞은 스펠링으로 이뤄진
단어를 따라가
미로 찾기

Word Puzzle

주어진 문장에
알맞은 단어를 쓰며
퍼즐 완성하기

Word Search 1

힌트를 보고
알맞은 그림을 찾아
쓰기 연습하기

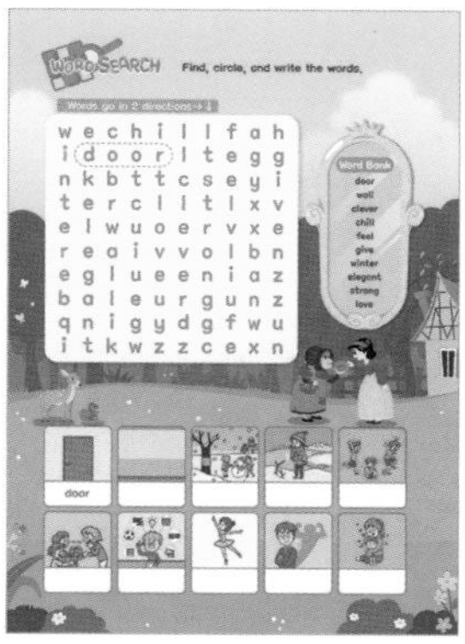

Word Search 2

다양한 알파벳 속
배운 단어를 찾아
쓰기 연습하기

복습 & 테스트

지금까지 배운 단어 정리하고, 테스트로 최종 점검!
뜯어서 쓰는 나만의 단어장까지!

Study Planner & Contents

Part 1

Day 01 Animals

망각 제로란?

※ 망각 제로는 [DAY 02]부터 시작합니다.

Is it a real bear?

Pop Quiz Choose and check the right words.

There's a person in a bear costume.

_______________으로 분장한 사람이 있어요.

- [x] 곰
- [ ] 코끼리

There are a zebra and an elephant too.

_______________과 코끼리도 있어요.

- [ ] 얼룩말
- [ ] 원숭이

Catch Up

Listen & Say Listen, say, and color.

Read & Write Write the **Basic Words** and **Jump Up Words.**

animal
동물

n

Let's go and see the animals.
동물들을 보러 가자.

animal

bear
곰

n

A bear is in the cave.
곰이 동굴 안에 있어요.

elephant
코끼리

n

An elephant is in the water.
코끼리가 물속에 있어요.

monkey
원숭이

A monkey is in the tree.
원숭이가 나무 위에 있어요.

n

zebra
얼룩말

A zebra is running.
얼룩말이 달리고 있어요.

n

escape
달아나다, 탈출하다

A rabbit tried to escape.
토끼는 달아나려고 했어요.

v

trace
추적하다, 흔적

We trace a tiger's paw prints.
우리는 호랑이의 발자국을 추적해요.

v n

hole
구멍

A mouse found a hole.
쥐가 구멍을 발견했어요.

n

Skill Up

A Choose and write the words.

monkey bear zebra

1 

bear

곰

2 

원숭이

3 

얼룩말

B Cross out, unscramble, and write the words.

1 코끼리 p e l m e a t n h — elephant

2 원숭이 n k a o m y e

3 달아나다, 탈출하다 s g c e a e p

4 동물 e n a m l i a

C Connect and fill in the blanks.

1 

2 

3 

A mouse found a hole.

쥐가 __________ 을 발견했어요.

An elephant is in the water.

코끼리 가 물속에 있어요.

We trace a tiger's paw prints.

우리는 호랑이의 발자국을 __________.

D Rearrange and write the sentences.

1 얼룩말이 달리고 있어요.

running | A zebra | is | .

A zebra is running.

2 곰이 동굴 안에 있어요.

A bear | is | the cave | in | .

Day 02

Body & Health

Check Up Read and check the words you don't know.

1차 복습

- [ ] animal
- [ ] bear
- [ ] elephant
- [ ] monkey
- [ ] zebra
- [ ] escape
- [ ] trace
- [ ] hole

※**망각 제로!** 1일 전 학습한 단어를 복습해요.

Word Tip

animal 동물 **bear** 곰 **elephant** 코끼리 **monkey** 원숭이

zebra 얼룩말 **escape** 달아나다, 탈출하다 **trace** 추적하다, 흔적 **hole** 구멍

Are you okay?

Pop Quiz Choose and check the right words.

Sally asks Rod if he hurt his back.

샐리는 로드에게 __________ 를 다쳤는지 물어요.

☐ 허리
☐ 무릎

Kiara thinks Rod should go to the hospital.

키아라는 로드가 __________ 에 가야 한다고 생각해요.

☐ 약
☐ 병원

Catch UP

Listen & Say **Listen, say, and color.**

Read & Write **Write the Basic Words and Jump Up Words.**

finger 손가락	**His finger is long.** 그의 손가락은 길어요.	n

back 허리, 등	**My back hurts.** 내 허리가 아파요.	n

knee 무릎	**A sore knee needs rest.** 아픈 무릎에는 휴식이 필요해요.	n

hospital
병원

n

A hospital has many doctors.
병원에는 많은 의사들이 있어요.

drug
약

n

This drug helps patients recover.
이 약은 환자의 회복을 도와요.

toe
발가락

n

My toes hurt a lot.
내 발가락이 아주 아파요.

examine
진찰하다,
조사하다

v

The doctor will examine you.
의사가 당신을 진찰할 거예요.

chin
턱

n

The doctor examined his chin.
의사가 그의 턱을 진찰했어요.

Skill UP

A Find, circle, and write the words.

1 

손가락

m f i n g e r n

finger

2 

무릎

s a k n e e o

3 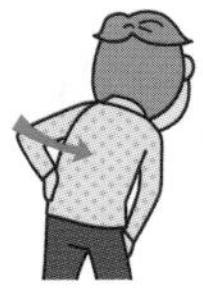

허리, 등

k d b a c k t

4 

턱

r f s c h i n g

B Choose and write the words.

toe hospital examine drug

1 발가락 toe

2 병원

3 약

4 진찰하다, 조사하다

C Unscramble and complete the sentences.

1 

병원에는 많은 의사들이 있어요.

p i h s o a l t

A hospital has many doctors.

2 

의사가 당신을 진찰할 거예요.

e a m i e x n

The doctor will ________ you.

3 

이 약은 환자의 회복을 도와요.

r u d g

This ________ helps patients recover.

D Choose and complete the sentences.

knee   toes   finger

1 내 발가락이 아주 아파요.

My toes hurt a lot.

2 아픈 무릎에는 휴식이 필요해요.

A sore ________ needs rest.

3 그의 손가락은 길어요.

His ________ is long.

Day 03

School

Check Up Read and check the words you don't know.

1차 복습

- [ ] finger
- [ ] back
- [ ] knee
- [ ] hospital
- [ ] drug
- [ ] toe
- [ ] examine
- [ ] chin

※ **망각 제로!** 1일 전 학습한 단어를 복습해요.

Word Tip

finger 손가락
back 허리, 등
knee 무릎
hospital 병원
drug 약
toe 발가락
examine 진찰하다, 조사하다
chin 턱

Dennis likes math.

Pop Quiz Choose and check the right words.

Math is Dennis's favorite subject.

__________은 데니스가 가장 좋아하는 과목이에요.

☐ 미술

☐ 수학

Dennis says he has a talent for math.

데니스는 자신이 수학에 __________이 있다고 말해요.

☐ 재능

☐ 과목

Catch Up

Listen & Say **Listen, say, and color.**

Read & Write **Write the Basic Words and Jump Up Words.**

art 미술	n I like art. 나는 미술을 좋아해요.	
math 수학	n We are learning shapes in math class. 우리는 수학 시간에 도형을 배우고 있어요.	
science 과학	n He likes science. 그는 과학을 좋아해요.	

music
음악

We like music. (n)
우리는 음악을 좋아해요.

subject
과목, 주제

What is your favorite subject? (n)
당신이 가장 좋아하는 과목이 무엇인가요?

solve
풀다,
해결하다

Let's solve the puzzle. (v)
퍼즐을 풀자.

talent
재능, 재주

She has different talents. (n)
그녀는 다양한 재능을 가지고 있어요.

favorite
매우 좋아하는

History is my favorite subject. (a)
역사는 내가 가장 좋아하는 과목이에요.

Skill UP

A Choose and write the words.

math science art

1 

수학

2 

미술

3 

과학

B Choose and write the words.

subject favorite solve music

1 음악

2 과목, 주제

3 풀다, 해결하다

4 매우 좋아하는

C Unscramble and complete the sentences.

1 

그녀는 다양한 재능을 가지고 있어요.

a n t e l t s

She has different ________.

2 

퍼즐을 풀자.

o s v e l

Let's ________ the puzzle.

3 

당신이 가장 좋아하는 과목이 무엇인가요?

u s b c e j t

What is your favorite ________?

D Rearrange and write the sentences.

1 그는 과학을 좋아해요.

likes | He | science | .

____

2 우리는 수학 시간에 도형을 배우고 있어요.

math class | are learning | in | shapes | We | .

____

Day 04

Communication

Check Up Read and check the words you don't know.

1차 복습

- [ ] art
- [ ] math
- [ ] science
- [ ] music
- [ ] subject
- [ ] solve
- [ ] talent
- [ ] favorite

2차 복습

- [ ] animal
- [ ] bear
- [ ] trace
- [ ] hole

※망각 제로! 1일 전 3일 전 학습한 단어를 복습해요.

Word Tip

art 미술
math 수학
science 과학
music 음악
subject 과목, 주제
solve 풀다, 해결하다
talent 재능, 재주
favorite 매우 좋아하는
animal 동물
bear 곰
trace 달아나다, 탈출하다
hole 구멍

Good luck, Kiara!

Pop Quiz Choose and check the right words.

Kiara will probably audition before experts.

키아라는 ______________ 들 앞에서 오디션을 볼 거예요.

- [ ] 전문가
- [ ] 말하다

Kiara will answer questions from the experts.

키아라는 전문가들의 질문에 ______________ 거예요.

- [ ] 대답하다
- [ ] 초대하다

Catch Up

Listen & Say Listen, say, and color.

Read & Write Write the **Basic Words** and **Jump Up Words.**

answer
대답하다

She answers the question.
그녀는 질문에 대답해요.

ask
묻다

He asks her name.
그가 그녀에게 이름을 물어요.

speak
말하다

I can speak English.
나는 영어로 말할 수 있어요.

invite
초대하다

v

They invite me to the party.
그들은 나를 파티에 초대해요.

listen
듣다

v

We listen to music.
우리는 음악을 들어요.

entire
전체의, 온

a

I want to hear the entire story.
나는 전체 이야기를 듣고 싶어요.

expert
전문가

n

She is a public speaking expert.
그녀는 연설 전문가예요.

wonder
궁금해하다

v

I wonder what my friend will say.
나는 내 친구가 뭐라고 말할지 궁금해요.

Skill UP

A Choose and write the words.

ask　　invite　　speak

1 

말하다

2 

초대하다

3 

묻다

B Cross out, unscramble, and write the words.

1 대답하다　s a n e w c r

2 전체의, 온　n t g e i e r

3 전문가　e p x e t r a

4 궁금해하다　v w n e r d o

C Connect and fill in the blanks.

1 

2 

3 

- I wonder what my friend will say.
  나는 내 친구가 뭐라고 말할지 ____________.

- She is a public speaking expert.
  그녀는 연설 ____________예요.

- We listen to music.
  우리는 음악을 ____________.

D Choose and complete the sentences.

entire	invite	speak

1 그들은 나를 파티에 초대해요.

They ____________ me to the party.

2 나는 전체 이야기를 듣고 싶어요.

I want to hear the ____________ story.

3 나는 영어로 말할 수 있어요.

I can ____________ English.

Day 05

Food & Drink

Check Up Read and check the words you don't know.

1차 복습

- [ ] answer
- [ ] ask
- [ ] speak
- [ ] invite
- [ ] listen
- [ ] entire
- [ ] expert
- [ ] wonder

2차 복습

- [ ] finger
- [ ] back
- [ ] examine
- [ ] chin

※망각 제로! 1일 전 3일 전 학습한 단어를 복습해요.

Word Tip

answer 대답하다	ask 묻다	speak 말하다	invite 초대하다
listen 듣다	entire 전체의, 온	expert 전문가	wonder 궁금해하다
finger 손가락	back 허리, 등	examine 진찰하다, 조사하다	chin 턱

Let's pick sweet strawberries!

Pop Quiz Choose and check the right words.

At first, Dennis was so hungry.

처음에 데니스는 너무 ____________요.

☐ 배부른

☐ 배고픈

Dennis says the strawberries are sweet.

데니스는 딸기가 ____________다고 말해요.

☐ 맛이 쓴

☐ 달콤한

Catch Up

Listen & Say Listen, say, and color.

Read & Write Write the **Basic Words** and **Jump Up Words**.

sweet 달콤한	I love eating sweet fruit. 나는 달콤한 과일을 먹는 것을 아주 좋아해요.	
full 배부른	I'm full after eating pizza. 나는 피자를 먹어서 배불러요.	
hungry 배고픈	I'm feeling hungry. 나는 배가 고파요.	

advise

충고하다

v

My mom advises me to eat vegetables.

엄마는 나에게 채소를 먹으라고 충고해요.

bake

굽다

v

Let's bake a cake together.

우리 같이 케이크를 굽자.

seal

밀봉하다

v

Can you seal the bag of chips?

과자 봉지를 밀봉해 줄 수 있나요?

bitter

맛이 쓴, 격렬한

a

The coffee tasted bitter.

그 커피는 맛이 썼어요.

tea

차, 찻잎

n

I like drinking tea.

나는 차 마시는 것을 좋아해요.

Skill UP

A Find, circle, and write the words.

1 

달콤한

c s w e e t d

2 

배부른

s h f u l l y

3 

굽다

h d b a k e k

4 

밀봉하다

r f s e a l k q

B Choose and write the words.

advise bitter tea hungry

1 배고픈

2 맛이 쓴, 격렬한

3 차, 찻잎

4 충고하다

C Unscramble and complete the sentences.

1

나는 배가 고파요.

I'm feeling ________.

u h n y r g

2

나는 차 마시는 것을 좋아해요.

I like drinking ________.

a e t

3

그 커피는 맛이 썼어요.

The coffee tasted ________.

i b t t r e

D Rearrange and write the sentences.

1 나는 피자를 먹어서 배불러요.

full | I'm | pizza | eating | after | .

2 나는 달콤한 과일을 먹는 것을 아주 좋아해요.

love | I | eating | fruit | sweet | .

WORD MAZE Follow the correctly spelled words.

animal 동물	bear 곰	elephant 코끼리	monkey 원숭이	zebra 얼룩말

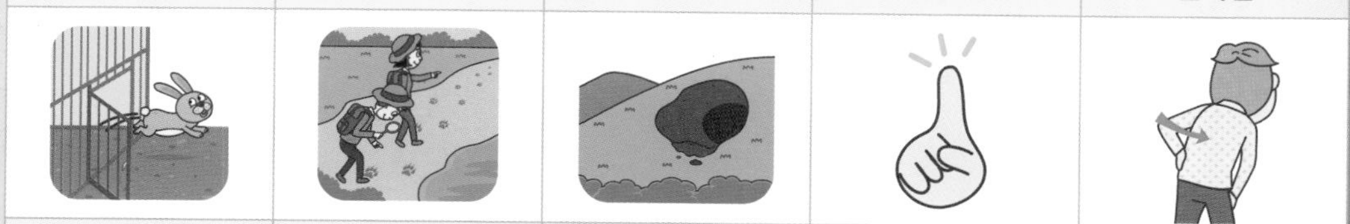

escape 달아나다, 탈출하다	trace 추적하다, 흔적	hole 구멍	finger 손가락	back 허리, 등

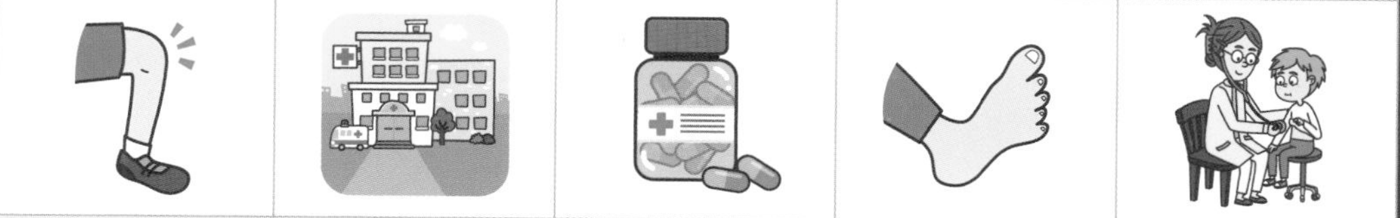

knee 무릎	hospital 병원	drug 약	toe 발가락	examine 진찰하다, 조사하다

chin 턱	art 미술	math 수학	science 과학	music 음악

subject 과목, 주제	solve 풀다, 해결하다	talent 재능, 재주	favorite 매우 좋아하는	answer 대답하다

ask 묻다	speak 말하다	invite 초대하다	listen 듣다	entire 전체의, 온

expert 전문가	wonder 궁금해하다	sweet 달콤한	full 배부른	hungry 배고픈

advise 충고하다	bake 굽다	seal 밀봉하다	bitter 맛이 쓴, 격렬한	tea 차, 찻잎

Review TEST

맞힌 개수 : ☐ / 40

1 animal		21 얼룩말	
2 bear		22 코끼리	
3 escape		23 추적하다, 흔적	
4 monkey		24 구멍	
5 finger		25 약	
6 back		26 발가락	
7 knee		27 병원	
8 examine		28 턱	
9 art		29 과목, 주제	
10 math		30 풀다, 해결하다	
11 science		31 재능, 재주	
12 music		32 매우 좋아하는	
13 answer		33 듣다	
14 ask		34 전체의, 온	
15 speak		35 전문가	
16 invite		36 궁금해하다	
17 sweet		37 굽다	
18 full		38 밀봉하다	
19 hungry		39 맛이 쓴, 격렬한	
20 advise		40 차, 찻잎	

Part 2

Day 06 Physical Space

Check Up Read and check the words you don't know.

1차 복습

- [ ] sweet
- [ ] full
- [ ] hungry
- [ ] advise
- [ ] bake
- [ ] seal
- [ ] bitter
- [ ] tea

2차 복습

- [ ] art
- [ ] math
- [ ] talent
- [ ] favorite

※ **망각 제로!** 1일 전 3일 전 학습한 단어를 복습해요.

Word Tip

sweet 달콤한	full 배부른	hungry 배고픈	advise 충고하다
bake 굽다	seal 밀봉하다	bitter 맛이 쓴, 격렬한	tea 차, 찻잎
art 미술	math 수학	talent 재능, 재주	favorite 매우 좋아하는

What a delicious house!

Pop Quiz Choose and check the right words.

Rod made the floor with wafers.

로드는 ___________ 을 웨이퍼로 만들었어요.

Rod made the walls with cookie sticks.

로드는 ___________ 을 막대 과자로 만들었어요.

☐ 바닥
☐ 창문
☐ 문
☐ 벽

Catch Up

Listen & Say Listen, say, and color.

Read & Write Write the **Basic Words** and **Jump Up Words.**

door
문

n

Knock on the door first.
문을 먼저 두드리세요.

floor
바닥, 층

n

The floor is cold.
바닥이 차가워요.

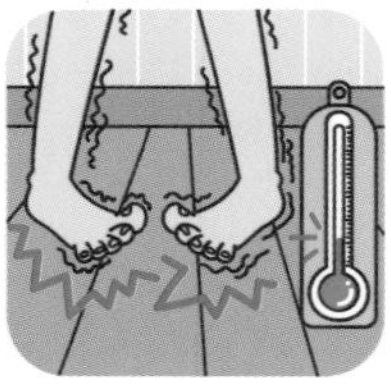

wall
벽

n

He hung a picture on the wall.
그는 벽에 그림을 걸었어요.

window
창문

The cat is looking out the window. ⓝ
고양이가 창문 밖을 내다보고 있어요.

stairs
계단

The dog likes to sit on the stairs. ⓝ
그 개는 계단에 앉는 것을 좋아해요.

passage
통로, 복도

Students walk through the passage. ⓝ
학생들은 통로를 통해 걸어가요.

actual
실제의

The actual size of the room is big. ⓐ
그 방의 실제 크기는 커요.

atmosphere
분위기, 대기

The atmosphere in the park is peaceful. ⓝ
공원의 분위기는 평화로워요.

Skill UP

A Choose and write the words.

floor window passage

1 

창문

2 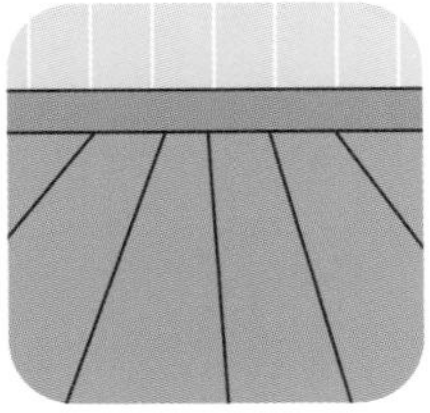

바닥, 층

3 

통로, 복도

B Cross out, unscramble, and write the words.

1 계단 s r n a s i t

2 문 r s o d o

3 벽 a w l l e

4 실제의 a u c a l d t

C Connect and fill in the blanks.

1 

2 

3 

He hung a picture on the wall.

그는 ____________에 그림을 걸었어요.

The dog likes to sit on the stairs.

그 개는 ____________에 앉는 것을 좋아해요.

Knock on the door first.

____________을 먼저 두드리세요.

D Choose and complete the sentences.

actual	window	floor

1 바닥이 차가워요.

The ____________ is cold.

2 그 방의 실제 크기는 커요.

The ____________ size of the room is big.

3 고양이가 창문 밖을 내다보고 있어요.

The cat is looking out the ____________.

Day 07 Seasons & Weather

Check Up Read and check the words you don't know.

1차 복습

- [ ] door
- [ ] floor
- [ ] wall
- [ ] window
- [ ] stairs
- [ ] passage
- [ ] actual
- [ ] atmosphere

2차 복습

- [ ] answer
- [ ] ask
- [ ] expert
- [ ] wonder

3차 복습

- [ ] elephant
- [ ] monkey
- [ ] zebra
- [ ] escape

※ 망각 제로! 1일 전 3일 전 7일 전 학습한 단어를 복습해요.

Word Tip

door 문
stairs 계단
answer 대답하다
elephant 코끼리

floor 바닥, 층
passage 통로, 복도
ask 묻다
monkey 원숭이

wall 벽
actual 실제의
expert 전문가
zebra 얼룩말

window 창문
atmosphere 분위기, 대기
wonder 궁금해하다
escape 달아나다, 탈출하다

It's spring.

Pop Quiz Choose and check the right words.

"It's spring," Kiara said.

키아라가 "__________이야."라고 말했어요.

☐ 겨울
☐ 봄

Sally likes summer and winter.

샐리는 __________과 겨울을 좋아해요.

☐ 여름
☐ 가을

Catch Up

Listen & Say Listen, say, and color.

Read & Write Write the **Basic Words** and **Jump Up Words.**

spring
봄

n

She is enjoying spring.

그녀는 봄을 즐기고 있어요.

summer
여름

n

I go to the beach in summer.

나는 여름에 해변에 가요.

fall
가을

n

He reads books in fall.

그는 가을에 책을 읽어요.

winter
겨울

n

We make a snowman in **winter**.
우리는 겨울에 눈사람을 만들어요.

season
계절

n

There are four **seasons** in Korea.
한국에는 사계절이 있어요.

chill
냉기, 오한

n

I feel a **chill** in the air.
나는 공기에서 차가움을 느껴요.

climate
기후

n

Polar bears live in cold **climates**.
북극곰은 추운 기후에서 살아요.

mild
온화한, 순한

a

The weather is **mild** today.
오늘은 날씨가 온화해요.

Skill UP

A Find, circle, and write the words.

1 

c s p r i n g d

봄

2 

k s u m m e r r

여름

3 

k d f a l l e e

가을

4 

w i n t e r y z

겨울

B Choose and write the words.

mild　chill　climate　season

1. 냉기, 오한
2. 온화한, 순한
3. 계절
4. 기후

C Unscramble and complete the sentences.

1 

나는 공기에서 차가움을 느껴요.

h c l i l

I feel a ____________ in the air.

2 

오늘은 날씨가 온화해요.

i d l m

The weather is ____________ today.

3 

한국에는 사계절이 있어요.

s a o e n s s

There are four ____________ in Korea.

D Rearrange and write the sentences.

1 그녀는 봄을 즐기고 있어요.

spring | She | is enjoying | .

2 우리는 겨울에 눈사람을 만들어요.

make | We | a snowman | winter | in | .

Day 08

Experiences

Check Up Read and check the words you don't know.

1차 복습

- [ ] spring
- [ ] summer
- [ ] fall
- [ ] winter
- [ ] season
- [ ] chill
- [ ] climate
- [ ] mild

2차 복습

- [ ] sweet
- [ ] full
- [ ] bitter
- [ ] tea

3차 복습

- [ ] knee
- [ ] hospital
- [ ] drug
- [ ] toe

※**망각 제로!** 1일 전 3일 전 7일 전 학습한 단어를 복습해요.

Word Tip

spring 봄	summer 여름	fall 가을	winter 겨울
season 계절	chill 냉기, 오한	climate 기후	mild 온화한, 순한
sweet 달콤한	full 배부른	bitter 맛이 쓴, 격렬한	tea 차, 찻잎
knee 무릎	hospital 병원	drug 약	toe 발가락

Sally and Kiara talk about a memory.

Pop Quiz Choose and check the right words.

Sally asks Kiara if she remembers that day.

샐리는 키아라가 그날을 ____________ 는지 물어요.

☐ 기억하다
☐ 허락하다

Kiara gave Sally a key ring that day.

그날 키아라는 샐리에게 열쇠고리를 ____________.

☐ 받다
☐ 주다

Catch Up

Listen & Say Listen, say, and color.

Read & Write Write the **Basic Words** and **Jump Up Words**.

feel
느끼다

I **feel** happy when I play.
나는 놀 때 행복을 느껴요.

get
받다, 구하다

I want to **get** ice cream.
아이스크림을 받고 싶어요.

give
주다

Let's **give** gifts to Mom.
엄마에게 선물을 드리자.

remember
기억하다

v

She remembers his name.
그녀는 그의 이름을 기억해요.

send
보내다

v

He sends an email.
그는 이메일을 보내요.

allow
허락하다

v

Mom will allow us to go on a trip.
엄마는 우리가 여행하는 것을 허락할 거예요.

precious
소중한, 귀중한

a

My toy is precious to me.
내 장난감은 나에게 소중해요.

experience
경험

n

Riding a bike is a fun experience.
자전거를 타는 것은 재미있는 경험이에요.

Skill UP

A Choose and write the words.

give get remember

1 

받다, 구하다

2 

기억하다

3 

주다

B Choose and write the words.

feel experience allow precious

1 느끼다

2 경험

3 소중한, 귀중한

4 허락하다

C Connect and fill in the blanks.

1 

2 

3 

I feel happy when I play.
나는 놀 때 행복을 ________.

He sends an email.
그는 이메일을 ________.

My toy is precious to me.
내 장난감은 나에게 ________요.

D Choose and complete the sentences.

experience give allow

1 엄마에게 선물을 드리자.

Let's ________ gifts to Mom.

2 엄마는 우리가 여행하는 것을 허락할 거예요.

Mom will ________ us to go on a trip.

3 자전거를 타는 것은 재미있는 경험이에요.

Riding a bike is a fun ________.

Day 09

Characteristics

Check Up Read and check the words you don't know.

1차 복습

- [ ] feel
- [ ] get
- [ ] give
- [ ] remember
- [ ] send
- [ ] allow
- [ ] precious
- [ ] experience

2차 복습

- [ ] door
- [ ] floor
- [ ] actual
- [ ] atmosphere

3차 복습

- [ ] science
- [ ] music
- [ ] subject
- [ ] solve

※망각 제로! 1일 전 3일 전 7일 전 학습한 단어를 복습해요.

Word Tip

feel 느끼다
send 보내다
door 문
science 과학
get 받다, 구하다
allow 허락하다
floor 바닥, 층
music 음악
give 주다
precious 소중한, 귀중한
actual 실제의
subject 과목, 주제
remember 기억하다
experience 경험
atmosphere 분위기, 대기
solve 풀다, 해결하다

Let me introduce my pet.

Pop Quiz Choose and check the right words.

Dennis thinks Max is clever.

데니스는 맥스가 ________ 다고 생각해요.

☐ 영리한

☐ 못생긴

Rod thinks Luna is elegant.

로드는 루나가 ________ 다고 생각해요.

☐ 뚱뚱한

☐ 우아한

Catch UP

Listen & Say Listen, say, and color.

Read & Write Write the **Basic Words** and **Jump Up Words.**

beautiful
아름다운

The flowers are beautiful.
꽃들이 아름다워요.

ugly
못생긴

The doll is ugly.
그 인형은 못생겼어요.

fat
뚱뚱한

A pig is fat.
돼지는 뚱뚱해요.

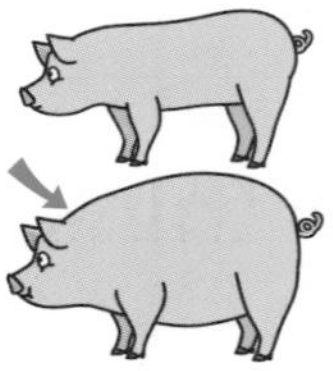

calm
침착한, 차분한

My dad is always calm.

우리 아빠는 항상 침착해요.

clever
영리한

My little brother is clever.

내 남동생은 영리해요.

brilliant
뛰어난, 훌륭한

My sister is a brilliant student.

내 여동생은 뛰어난 학생이에요.

elegant
우아한

The ballerina is very elegant.

발레리나는 매우 우아해요.

loyal
충성스러운

Dogs are loyal to their owners.

개들은 주인에게 충성스러워요.

Skill UP

A Choose and write the words.

ugly   loyal   clever

1 

영리한

2 

못생긴

3 

충성스러운

B Cross out, unscramble, and write the words.

1 침착한, 차분한 — r l a m c

2 아름다운 — b a e f l t i u x u

3 뛰어난, 훌륭한 — b l l i n r e a t i

4 우아한 — l e g a u e n t

C Connect and fill in the blanks.

1. 

A pig is fat.

돼지는 ____________ 요.

2. 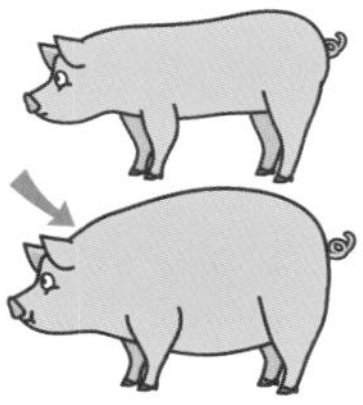

The ballerina is very elegant.

발레리나는 매우 ____________ 요.

3. 

The flowers are beautiful.

꽃이 ____________ 요.

D Rearrange and write the sentences.

1. 우리 아빠는 항상 침착해요.

calm | My | is always | dad | .

2. 내 남동생은 영리해요.

brother | My | little | clever | is | .

Day 10 Personality & Characteristics

Check Up Read and check the words you don't know.

1차 복습

- [ ] beautiful
- [ ] ugly
- [ ] fat
- [ ] calm
- [ ] clever
- [ ] brilliant
- [ ] elegant
- [ ] loyal

2차 복습

- [ ] spring
- [ ] summer
- [ ] climate
- [ ] mild

3차 복습

- [ ] speak
- [ ] invite
- [ ] listen
- [ ] entire

※망각 제로! 1일 전 3일 전 7일 전 학습한 단어를 복습해요.

Word Tip

beautiful 아름다운	ugly 못생긴	fat 뚱뚱한	calm 침착한, 차분한
clever 영리한	brilliant 뛰어난, 훌륭한	elegant 우아한	loyal 충성스러운
spring 봄	summer 여름	climate 기후	mild 온화한, 순한
speak 말하다	invite 초대하다	listen 듣다	entire 전체의, 온

I like the way I am.

Pop Quiz Choose and check the right words.

Rod wants to be strong.

로드는 ____________지고 싶어해요.

☐ 강한
☐ 약한

Kiara wants to be smart.

키아라는 ____________지고 싶어해요.

☐ 똑똑한
☐ 따분한

Catch Up

Listen & Say — Listen, say, and color.

Read & Write — Write the Basic Words and Jump Up Words.

strong
강한

ⓐ He has a strong personality.
그는 강한 성격을 가지고 있어요.

weak
약한

ⓐ She is emotionally weak.
그녀는 감정적으로 약해요.

love
사랑하다

ⓥ My mom loves me.
우리 엄마는 나를 사랑해요.

a

boring
따분한, 지루한

He is a boring person.

그는 따분한 사람이에요.

a

smart
똑똑한

My puppy is smart.

내 강아지는 똑똑해요.

n

skill
기술, 기량

She has good communication skills.

그녀는 좋은 의사소통 기술을 가지고 있어요.

v

knock
노크하다, 두드리다

He always knocks before entering rooms.

그는 방에 들어가기 전에 항상 노크해요.

a n

patient
인내심 있는, 환자

My grandma is very patient.

우리 할머니는 매우 인내심이 있어요.

Skill UP

A Find, circle, and write the words.

1 

약한

s g w e a k r z

2 

노크하다, 두드리다

k s k n o c k g

3 

강한

b s t r o n g e

4 

사랑하다

d l o v e w k w

B Choose and write the words.

skill　patient　smart　boring

1 따분한, 지루한

2 기술, 기량

3 인내심 있는, 환자

4 똑똑한

C Unscramble and complete the sentences.

1 

내 강아지는 똑똑해요.

a r s m t

My puppy is ________.

2 

그는 따분한 사람이에요.

i r b o g n

He is a ________ person.

3 

우리 할머니는 매우 인내심이 있어요.

a p t e t i n

My grandma is very ________.

D Choose and complete the sentences.

weak	skills	strong

1 그는 강한 성격을 가지고 있어요.

He has a ________ personality.

2 그녀는 감정적으로 약해요.

She is emotionally ________.

3 그녀는 좋은 의사소통 기술을 가지고 있어요.

She has good communication ________.

WORD SEARCH

Find, circle, and write the words.

Words go in 2 directions → ↓

w	e	c	h	i	l	l	f	a	h
i	d	o	o	r	l	t	e	g	g
n	k	b	t	t	c	s	e	y	i
t	e	r	c	l	l	t	l	x	v
e	l	w	u	o	e	r	v	x	e
r	e	a	i	v	v	o	l	b	n
e	g	l	u	e	e	n	i	a	z
b	a	l	e	u	r	g	u	n	z
q	n	i	g	y	d	g	f	w	u
i	t	k	w	z	z	c	e	x	n

Word Bank

door
wall
clever
chill
feel
give
winter
elegant
strong
love

door

Day 06~10

door 문	floor 바닥, 층	wall 벽	window 창문	stairs 계단

passage 통로, 복도	actual 실제의	atmosphere 분위기, 대기	spring 봄	summer 여름

fall 가을	winter 겨울	season 계절	chill 냉기, 오한	climate 기후

mild 온화한, 순한	feel 느끼다	get 받다, 구하다	give 주다	remember 기억하다

send 보내다	allow 허락하다	precious 소중한, 귀중한	experience 경험	beautiful 아름다운

ugly 못생긴	fat 뚱뚱한	calm 침착한, 차분한	clever 영리한	brilliant 뛰어난, 훌륭한

elegant 우아한	loyal 충성스러운	strong 강한	weak 약한	love 사랑하다

boring 따분한, 지루한	smart 똑똑한	skill 기술, 기량	knock 노크하다, 두드리다	patient 인내심 있는, 환자

Review TEST

맞힌 개수 : ☐ /40

1 door		21 계단	
2 floor		22 통로, 복도	
3 wall		23 실제의	
4 window		24 분위기, 대기	
5 spring		25 계절	
6 summer		26 냉기, 오한	
7 fall		27 기후	
8 winter		28 온화한, 순한	
9 feel		29 보내다	
10 get		30 허락하다	
11 give		31 소중한, 귀중한	
12 remember		32 경험	
13 beautiful		33 영리한	
14 ugly		34 뛰어난, 훌륭한	
15 fat		35 우아한	
16 calm		36 충성스러운	
17 strong		37 똑똑한	
18 weak		38 기술, 기량	
19 love		39 노크하다, 두드리다	
20 boring		40 인내심 있는, 환자	

Part 3

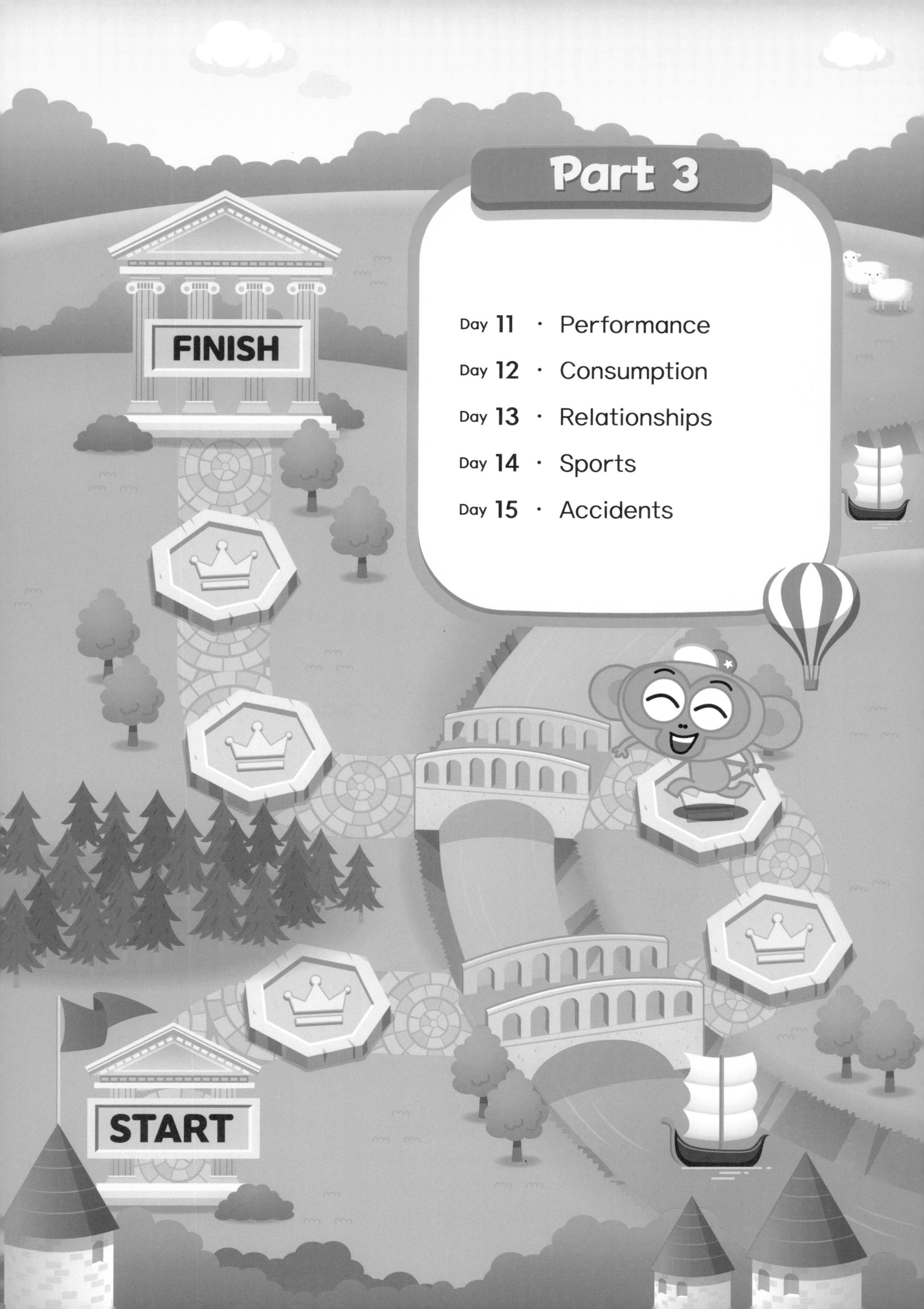

Day 11

Performance

Check Up Read and check the words you don't know.

1차 복습

- [ ] strong
- [ ] weak
- [ ] love
- [ ] boring
- [ ] smart
- [ ] skill
- [ ] knock
- [ ] patient

2차 복습

- [ ] feel
- [ ] get
- [ ] precious
- [ ] experience

3차 복습

- [ ] hungry
- [ ] advise
- [ ] bake
- [ ] seal

※ **망각 제로!** 1일 전 3일 전 7일 전 학습한 단어를 복습해요.

Word Tip

strong 강한	weak 약한	love 사랑하다	boring 따분한, 지루한
smart 똑똑한	skill 기술, 기량	knock 노크하다, 두드리다	patient 인내심 있는, 환자
feel 느끼다	get 받다, 구하다	precious 소중한, 귀중한	experience 경험
hungry 배고픈	advise 충고하다	bake 굽다	seal 밀봉하다

What a fantastic voice!

Pop Quiz Choose and check the right words.

Camila thinks he has a fantastic voice.

카밀라는 그가 ____________ 목소리를 가졌다고 생각해요.

☐ 최고의

☐ 환상적인

Lucia thinks he's a music genius.

루시아는 그가 음악 ____________ 라고 생각해요.

☐ 천재

☐ 노래

Catch Up

Listen & Say Listen, say, and color.

Read & Write Write the **Basic Words** and **Jump Up Words.**

background
배경

n

Background music starts playing.
배경 음악이 재생되기 시작해요.

picture
그림, 사진

n

My sister draws a picture.
내 여동생이 그림을 그려요.

fantastic
환상적인

a

The play was fantastic.
그 연극은 환상적이었어요.

song
노래

n

The song was beautiful.
그 노래는 아름다웠어요.

tell
이야기를 하다, 말하다

v

My grandma tells us a story.
우리 할머니는 우리에게 이야기를 해주세요.

stage
무대, 단계

n

The stage was set.
무대가 준비되었어요.

superb
대단히 훌륭한, 최고의

a

The performance was superb.
그 공연은 대단히 훌륭했어요.

genius
천재, 천재성

n

He is a music genius.
그는 음악 천재예요.

Skill UP

A Choose and write the words.

picture superb stage

1 

그림, 사진

2 

무대, 단계

3 

대단히 훌륭한, 최고의

B Choose and write the words.

tell background genius fantastic

1 환상적인

2 이야기를 하다, 말하다

3 천재, 천재성

4 배경

C Connect and fill in the blanks.

1 

2 

3 

The song was beautiful.
그 ____________는 아름다웠어요.

The play was fantastic.
그 연극은 ______________요.

He is a music genius.
그는 음악 ____________예요.

D Choose and complete the sentences.

picture   Background   stage

1 내 여동생이 그림을 그려요.

My sister draws a ____________.

2 무대가 준비되었어요.

The ____________ was set.

3 배경 음악이 재생되기 시작해요.

____________________ music starts playing.

Day 12
Consumption

Check Up Read and check the words you don't know.

1차 복습

- [ ] background
- [ ] picture
- [ ] fantastic
- [ ] song
- [ ] tell
- [ ] stage
- [ ] superb
- [ ] genius

2차 복습

- [ ] elegant
- [ ] clever
- [ ] ugly
- [ ] fat

3차 복습

- [ ] wall
- [ ] window
- [ ] actual
- [ ] door

※망각 제로! 1일 전 3일 전 7일 전 학습한 단어를 복습해요.

Word Tip

background 배경
tell 이야기를 하다, 말하다
elegant 우아한
wall 벽
picture 그림, 사진
stage 무대, 단계
clever 영리한
window 창문
fantastic 환상적인
superb 대단히 훌륭한, 최고의
ugly 못생긴
actual 실제의
song 노래
genius 천재, 천재성
fat 뚱뚱한
door 문

It's a bargain!

Pop Quiz Choose and check the right words.

Gelato is on sale for 50% off.

젤라또가 50% 할인 __________ 중이에요.

☐ 판매
☐ 동전

Kiara says it's an expensive ice cream.

키아라는 그것이 __________ 아이스크림이라고 말해요.

☐ 비싼
☐ 싼

Catch Up

Listen & Say Listen, say, and color.

Read & Write Write the **Basic Words** and **Jump Up Words.**

cheap
(값이) 싼

ⓐ
This bag is cheap.
이 가방은 싸요.

expensive
비싼

ⓐ
These shoes are expensive.
이 신발은 비싸요.

pay
지불하다, 내다

ⓥ
They have to pay.
그들은 돈을 내야 해요.

coin
동전

n

I have many coins.
나는 많은 동전을 가지고 있어요.

sale
판매

n

New products are for sale.
신제품들이 판매 중이에요.

bargain
할인한 물건,
흥정

n

It's a bargain price.
그것은 할인한 물건 가격이에요.

dash
서둘러 가다,
돌진

v n

People dash to the shop.
사람들이 가게로 서둘러 가요.

credit
외상,
신용 거래

n

He bought it on credit.
그는 그것을 외상으로 샀어요.

Skill UP

A Find, circle, and write the words.

1 

scheapyu

(값이) 싼

2 

aebnpayk

지불하다, 내다

3 

jcoingel

동전

4 

qovsalew

판매

B Choose and write the words.

dash	credit	expensive	cheap

1 비싼

2 (값이) 싼

3 서둘러 가다, 돌진

4 외상, 신용 거래

C Unscramble and complete the sentences.

1 

그것은 할인한 물건 가격이에요.

g r b a n i a

It's a ______________ price.

2 

이 신발은 비싸요.

x p n e v e s i e

These shoes are ______________.

3 

사람들이 가게로 서둘러 가요.

a h d s

People ______________ to the shop.

D Rearrange and write the sentences.

1 신제품들이 판매 중이에요.

are | for | New products | sale | .

____

2 그는 그것을 외상으로 샀어요.

bought | He | it | credit | on | .

____

Day 13

Relationships

Check Up Read and check the words you don't know.

1차 복습

- [ ] cheap
- [ ] expensive
- [ ] pay
- [ ] coin
- [ ] sale
- [ ] bargain
- [ ] dash
- [ ] credit

2차 복습

- [ ] strong
- [ ] weak
- [ ] knock
- [ ] patient

3차 복습

- [ ] fall
- [ ] winter
- [ ] season
- [ ] chill

※**망각 제로!** 1일 전 3일 전 7일 전 학습한 단어를 복습해요.

Word Tip

cheap (값이) 싼
expensive 비싼
pay 지불하다, 내다
coin 동전
sale 판매
bargain 할인한 물건, 흥정
dash 서둘러 가다, 돌진
credit 외상, 신용 거래
strong 강한
weak 약한
knock 노크하다, 두드리다
patient 인내심 있는, 환자
fall 가을
winter 겨울
season 계절
chill 냉기, 오한

Happy anniversary!

Pop Quiz Choose and check the right words.

They are preparing a surprise party.

그들은 ＿＿＿＿＿＿＿ 파티를 준비하고 있어요.

- ☐ 기념일
- ☐ 깜짝 놀라게 하기

Some of the friends are decorating a cake.

＿＿＿＿＿＿＿ 중 몇 명은 케이크를 장식하고 있어요.

- ☐ 전통
- ☐ 친구

Catch Up

Listen & Say Listen, say, and color.

Read & Write Write the Basic Words and Jump Up Words.

father
아버지

n

Father's birthday is today!

아버지의 생신이 오늘이에요!

mother
어머니

n

My mother baked a cake.

우리 어머니는 케이크를 구웠어요.

parents
부모님

n

I love my parents.

나는 우리 부모님을 사랑해요.

friend
친구

She is a good friend.
그녀는 좋은 친구예요.

n

birthday
생일

Today is my birthday.
오늘은 내 생일이에요.

n

tradition
전통

We follow that tradition.
우리는 그 전통을 따라요.

n

anniversary
기념일

Today is our wedding anniversary.
오늘은 우리의 결혼기념일이에요.

n

surprise
놀라움,
깜짝 놀라게 하기

The party was a big surprise.
그 파티는 큰 놀라움이었어요.

n

Skill UP

A Choose and write the words.

friend   father   parents

1

아버지

2

친구

3

부모님

B Cross out, unscramble, and write the words.

1 어머니 — j m h r o e t

2 놀라움, 깜짝 놀라게 하기 — s q r u p e r s i

3 생일 — d b g a i h t y r

4 전통 — t i t d a k o r n i

C Connect and fill in the blanks.

❶ 

❷ 

❸ 

• Today is our wedding anniversary.

오늘은 우리의 결혼 __________ 이에요.

• Today is my birthday.

오늘은 내 __________ 이에요.

• The party was a big surprise.

그 파티는 큰 __________ 이었어요.

D Choose and complete the sentences.

mother　　parents　　tradition

❶ 우리 어머니는 케이크를 구웠어요.

My __________ baked a cake.

❷ 나는 우리 부모님을 사랑해요.

I love my __________.

❸ 우리는 그 전통을 따라요.

We follow that __________.

Day 14

Sports

Check Up Read and check the words you don't know.

1차 복습

- [ ] father
- [ ] mother
- [ ] parents
- [ ] friend
- [ ] birthday
- [ ] tradition
- [ ] anniversary
- [ ] surprise

2차 복습

- [ ] background
- [ ] picture
- [ ] superb
- [ ] genius

3차 복습

- [ ] give
- [ ] remember
- [ ] send
- [ ] allow

※**망각 제로!** 1일 전 3일 전 7일 전 학습한 단어를 복습해요.

Word Tip

father 아버지
mother 어머니
parents 부모님
friend 친구
birthday 생일
tradition 전통
anniversary 기념일
surprise 놀라움, 깜짝 놀라게 하기
background 배경
picture 그림, 사진
superb 대단히 훌륭한, 최고의
genius 천재, 천재성
give 주다
remember 기억하다
send 보내다
allow 허락하다

We lost the game.

Pop Quiz Choose and check the right words.

Dennis's body was not in good condition.

데니스의 몸은 좋은 __________가 아니었어요.

☐ 야구
☐ 상태

Mong suggests exercising first before eating.

몽은 먹기 전에 __________부터 하자고 제안해요.

☐ 운동하다
☐ 경쟁하다

Catch UP

Listen & Say Listen, say, and color.

Read & Write Write the **Basic Words** and **Jump Up Words.**

baseball 야구	**We can play baseball.** 우리는 야구를 할 수 있어요.	
basketball 농구	**We love playing basketball.** 우리는 농구하는 것을 아주 좋아해요.	
soccer 축구	**Soccer is our favorite sport.** 축구는 우리가 가장 좋아하는 스포츠예요.	

condition
(경기자의) 컨디션, 상태, 조건

ⓝ The players are in good condition.

그 선수들은 컨디션이 좋아요.

exercise
운동하다, 운동

ⓥⓝ We exercise every day.

우리는 매일 운동해요.

athlete
운동선수

ⓝ She is a talented athlete.

그녀는 재능 있는 운동선수예요.

compete
경쟁하다, 겨루다

ⓥ We compete in tournaments.

우리는 토너먼트에서 경쟁해요.

defeat
이기다, (상대를) 패배시키다

ⓥ We can defeat that soccer team.

우리는 그 축구팀을 이길 수 있어요.

Skill Up

A Find, circle, and write the words.

1 

e h s o c c e r g

축구

2 

n b a s e b a l l

야구

3 

e a t h l e t e f

운동선수

4 

e x e r c i s e t

운동하다, 운동

B Choose and write the words.

defeat basketball condition compete

1 이기다, (상대를) 패배시키다

2 (경기자의) 컨디션, 상태, 조건

3 농구

4 경쟁하다, 겨루다

C Connect and fill in the blanks.

1 

2 

3 

We love playing basketball.

우리는 ____________ 하는 것을 아주 좋아해요.

We compete in tournaments.

우리는 토너먼트에서 ____________.

The players are in good condition.

그 선수들은 ____________ 이 좋아요.

D Rearrange and write the sentences.

1 우리는 매일 운동해요.

every day | exercise | We | .

2 축구는 우리가 가장 좋아하는 스포츠예요.

Soccer | our | is | sport | favorite | .

Day 15

Accidents

Check Up Read and check the words you don't know.

1차 복습

- [ ] baseball
- [ ] basketball
- [ ] exercise
- [ ] condition
- [ ] soccer
- [ ] athlete
- [ ] compete
- [ ] defeat

2차 복습

- [ ] cheap
- [ ] expensive
- [ ] dash
- [ ] credit

3차 복습

- [ ] fat
- [ ] calm
- [ ] clever
- [ ] brilliant

※망각 제로! 1일 전 3일 전 7일 전 학습한 단어를 복습해요.

Word Tip

baseball 야구
soccer 축구
cheap (값이) 싼
fat 뚱뚱한
basketball 농구
athlete 운동선수
expensive 비싼
calm 침착한, 차분한
exercise 운동하다, 운동
compete 경쟁하다, 겨루다
dash 서둘러 가다, 돌진
clever 영리한
condition (경기자의) 컨디션, 상태, 조건
defeat 이기다, (상대를) 패배시키다
credit 외상, 신용 거래
brilliant 뛰어난, 훌륭한

Don't ride a bicycle on a rainy day!

Pop Quiz Choose and check the right words.

Dennis's mom says the roads are slippery.

데니스의 엄마는 __________이 미끄럽다고 말해요.

☐ 길
☐ 안개

Dennis's mom worries he might have an accident.

데니스의 엄마는 데니스에게 __________가 날지도 모른다고 걱정해요.

☐ 위험
☐ 사고

Catch Up

Listen & Say Listen, say, and color.

Read & Write Write the Basic Words and Jump Up Words.

road
도로, 길

n

There are many cars on the road.
도로에 많은 차들이 있어요.

bicycle
자전거

n

I ride my bicycle.
나는 자전거를 타요.

danger
위험

n

The sign says danger.
그 표지판은 위험을 나타내요.

fog 안개

n

The fog is thick.

안개가 짙어요.

accident 사고

n

He had a car accident.

그는 교통사고를 당했어요.

prevent 예방하다, 막다

v

You can prevent a cold.

당신은 감기를 예방할 수 있어요.

scare 겁주다, 겁먹다

v

The noise scared me.

그 소음은 나를 겁먹게 했어요.

avoid 피하다

v

We should avoid danger.

우리는 위험을 피해야 해요.

Skill UP

A Choose and write the words.

fog scare bicycle

1 

자전거

2 

안개

3 

겁주다, 겁먹다

B Cross out, unscramble, and write the words.

1 피하다 a m i v o d

2 사고 c a d u n t i c e

3 위험 d b g n a r e

4 예방하다, 막다 e v p d r n e t

C Unscramble and complete the sentences.

1 

도로에 많은 차들이 있어요.

a r d o

There are many cars on the ________.

2 

그는 교통사고를 당했어요.

a i c d c e n t

He had a car ____________.

3 

그 표지판은 위험을 나타내요.

d g n a r e

The sign says __________.

D Choose and complete the sentences.

bicycle	fog	avoid

1 안개가 짙어요.

The __________ is thick.

2 나는 자전거를 타요.

I ride my __________.

3 우리는 위험을 피해야 해요.

We should __________ danger.

WORD PUZZLE

Complete the word puzzle.

Word Bank

- road
- tell
- song
- mother
- sale
- friend
- pay
- soccer
- fog
- basketball

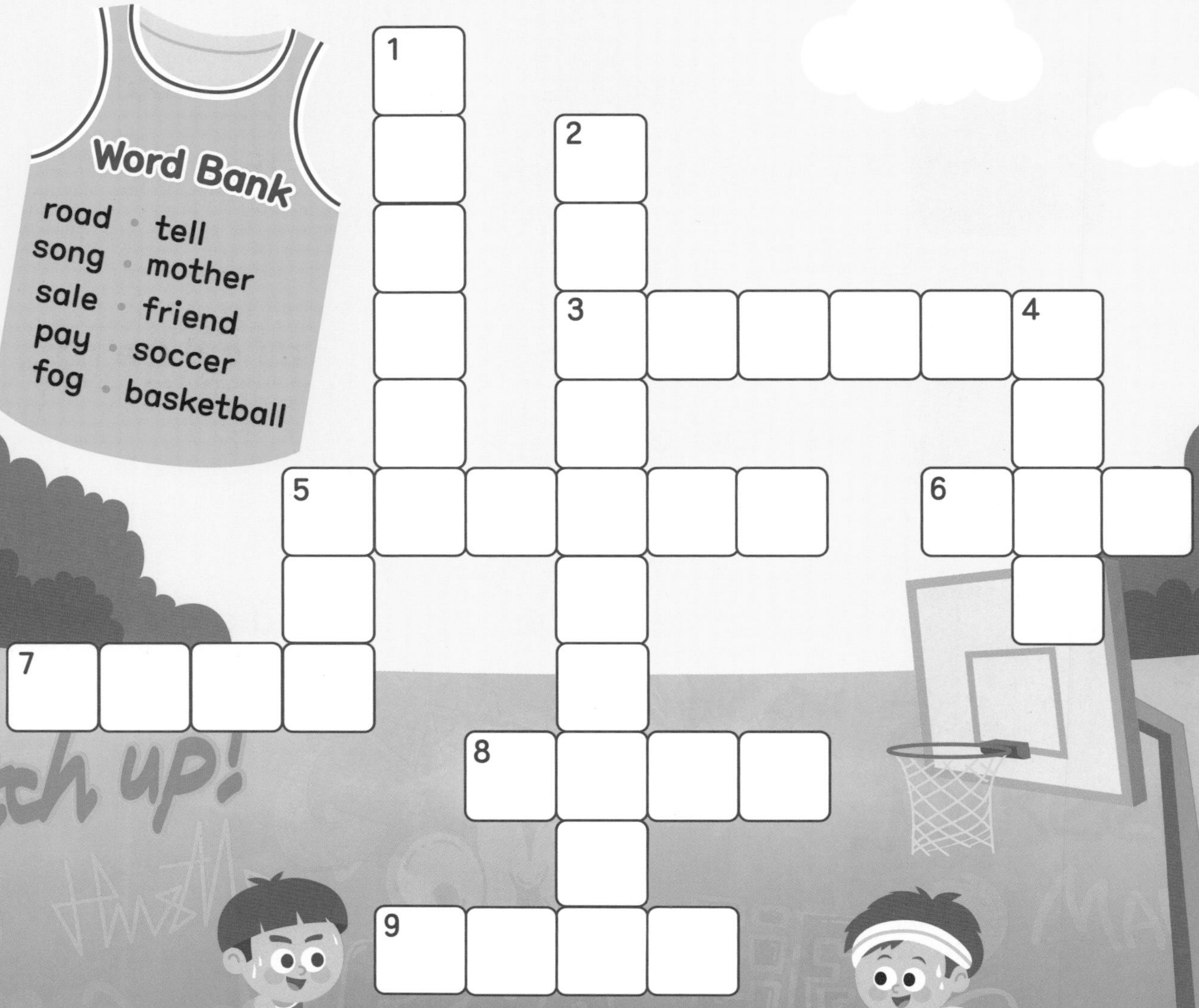

ACROSS

③

⑤

⑥

⑦

⑧

⑨

DOWN

①

②

④

⑤

Day 11~15

background 배경

picture 그림, 사진

fantastic 환상적인

song 노래

tell 이야기를 하다, 말하다

stage 무대, 단계

superb 대단히 훌륭한, 최고의

genius 천재, 천재성

cheap (값이) 싼

expensive 비싼

pay 지불하다, 내다

coin 동전

sale 판매

bargain 할인한 물건, 흥정

dash 서둘러 가다, 돌진

credit 외상, 신용 거래

father 아버지

mother 어머니

parents 부모님

friend 친구

birthday 생일

tradition 전통

anniversary 기념일

surprise 놀라움, 깜짝 놀라게 하기

baseball 야구

basketball 농구

soccer 축구

condition (경기자의) 컨디션, 상태, 조건

exercise 운동하다, 운동

athlete 운동선수

compete 경쟁하다, 겨루다

defeat 이기다, (상대를) 패배시키다

road 도로, 길

bicycle 자전거

danger 위험

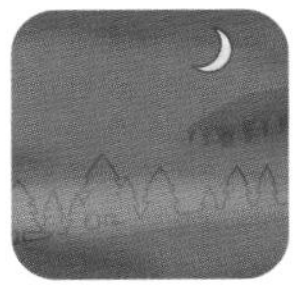

fog 안개

accident 사고

prevent 예방하다, 막다

scare 겁주다, 겁먹다

avoid 피하다

Review TEST

맞힌 개수 :   / 40

1 tell		21 배경	
2 picture		22 무대, 단계	
3 fantastic		23 노래	
4 superb		24 천재, 천재성	
5 cheap		25 판매	
6 expensive		26 할인한 물건, 흥정	
7 pay		27 서둘러 가다, 돌진	
8 coin		28 외상, 신용 거래	
9 father		29 생일	
10 mother		30 전통	
11 parents		31 기념일	
12 surprise		32 친구	
13 baseball		33 운동하다, 운동	
14 basketball		34 운동선수	
15 defeat		35 경쟁하다, 겨루다	
16 condition		36 축구	
17 road		37 사고	
18 bicycle		38 예방하다, 막다	
19 danger		39 겁주다, 겁먹다	
20 fog		40 피하다	

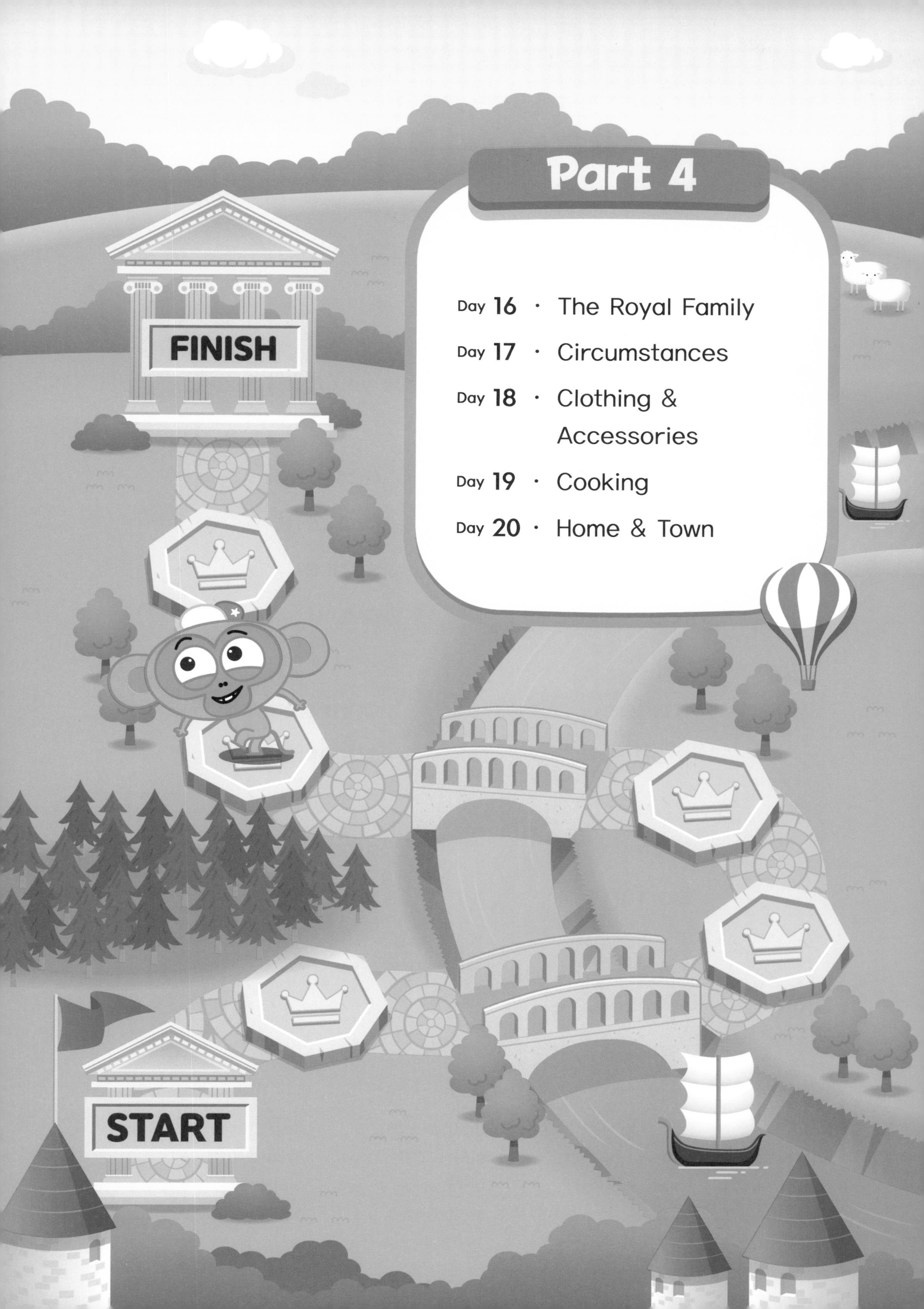

Part 4

Day 16

The Royal Family

Check Up Read and check the words you don't know.

1차 복습

- [ ] road
- [ ] bicycle
- [ ] danger
- [ ] fog
- [ ] accident
- [ ] prevent
- [ ] scare
- [ ] avoid

2차 복습

- [ ] father
- [ ] mother
- [ ] anniversary
- [ ] surprise

3차 복습

- [ ] love
- [ ] boring
- [ ] smart
- [ ] skill

※**망각 제로!** 1일 전 3일 전 7일 전 학습한 단어를 복습해요.

Word Tip

road 도로, 길
bicycle 자전거
danger 위험
fog 안개
accident 사고
prevent 예방하다, 막다
scare 겁주다, 겁먹다
avoid 피하다
father 아버지
mother 어머니
anniversary 기념일
surprise 놀라움, 깜짝 놀라게 하기
love 사랑하다
boring 따분한, 지루한
smart 똑똑한
skill 기술, 기량

Let's take a picture!

Pop Quiz Choose and check the right words.

Sally likes the princess costume.

샐리는 ________ 복장을 맘에 들어해요.

☐ 공주

☐ 왕자

Dennis dressed up as a wicked queen.

데니스는 못된 ________처럼 입었어요.

☐ 왕

☐ 여왕

Catch Up

Listen & Say Listen, say, and color.

Read & Write Write the Basic Words and Jump Up Words.

king 왕	n The king looks tired. 왕이 피곤해 보여요.

queen 여왕	n The queen wears a beautiful dress. 여왕은 아름다운 드레스를 입어요.

prince 왕자	n The prince looks handsome. 왕자는 잘생겨 보여요.

princess
공주

The princess looks pretty. (n)
공주는 예뻐 보여요.

castle
성

They live in a castle. (n)
그들은 성에 살아요.

treasure
보물

The treasure is in the castle. (n)
그 보물은 성 안에 있어요.

coast
해안

The place is near the coast. (n)
그 장소는 해안 근처에 있어요.

locate
(특정 위치에)
두다

The king will locate his guards. (v)
왕은 경비병을 배치할 거예요.

Skill UP

A Find, circle, and write the words.

1 

왕

yuwkingz

2 

왕자

jsprince

3 

성

bkcastle

4 

여왕

lfqueeng

B Choose and write the words.

princess coast locate treasure

1 공주

2 해안

3 보물

4 (특정 위치에) 두다

C Connect and fill in the blanks.

1 

2 

3 

- The princess looks pretty.
  ______ 는 예뻐 보여요.
- The place is near the coast.
  그 장소는 ______ 근처에 있어요.
- The treasure is in the castle.
  그 ______ 은 성 안에 있어요.

D Rearrange and write the sentences.

1 그들은 성에 살아요.

in | live | They | a castle | .

2 왕은 경비병을 배치할 거예요.

locate | The king | will | his guards | .

Day 17 Circumstances

Check Up Read and check the words you don't know.

1차 복습

- [ ] king
- [ ] queen
- [ ] prince
- [ ] princess
- [ ] castle
- [ ] treasure
- [ ] coast
- [ ] locate

2차 복습

- [ ] baseball
- [ ] basketball
- [ ] compete
- [ ] defeat

3차 복습

- [ ] fantastic
- [ ] song
- [ ] tell
- [ ] stage

※ **망각 제로!** 1일 전 3일 전 7일 전 학습한 단어를 복습해요.

Word Tip

king 왕	**queen** 여왕	**prince** 왕자	**princess** 공주
castle 성	**treasure** 보물	**coast** 해안	**locate** (특정 위치에) 두다
baseball 야구	**basketball** 농구	**compete** 경쟁하다, 겨루다	**defeat** 이기다, (상대를) 패배시키다
fantastic 환상적인	**song** 노래	**tell** 이야기를 하다, 말하다	**stage** 무대, 단계

Oops, my mistake!

Pop Quiz Choose and check the right words.

A group of kids is playing with blocks.

한 ____________의 아이들이 블록 놀이를 하고 있어요.

- ☐ 무리, 집단
- ☐ 소리, 소음

Dennis asks if there's a problem.

데니스는 무슨 ____________가 있는지 물어요.

- ☐ 문제
- ☐ 나이

Catch Up

Listen & Say Listen, say, and color.

Read & Write Write the **Basic Words** and **Jump Up Words.**

age
나이

n

My age is ten.
내 나이는 10살이에요.

problem
문제

n

I can't solve this problem.
나는 이 문제를 해결할 수 없어요.

group
그룹, 무리, 집단

n

I made a study group.
나는 스터디 그룹을 만들었어요.

noise
소리, 소음

n

A siren makes a loud **noise**.
사이렌은 큰 소리를 내요.

guy
남자, 사람

n

He is a really nice **guy**.
그는 정말 좋은 남자예요.

mistake
실수, 잘못,
오해하다

n v

I made a big **mistake**.
나는 큰 실수를 했어요.

disturb
방해하다

v

The noise **disturbs** the group.
소음이 그 그룹을 방해해요.

endure
견디다, 참다

v

I can't **endure** the heat.
나는 더위를 견딜 수 없어요.

Skill UP

A Choose and write the words.

guy　　disturb　　group

1

그룹, 무리, 집단

2

남자, 사람

3

방해하다

B Cross out, unscramble, and write the words.

1 소리, 소음　　n u i s o e

2 실수, 잘못, 오해하다　　t a m g s i e k

3 견디다, 참다　　u e n g d r e

4 문제　　p r b d e m l o

C Unscramble and complete the sentences.

1 

내 나이는 10살이에요.

e g a

My ________ is ten.

2 

사이렌은 큰 소리를 내요.

o i s n e

A siren makes a loud ________.

3 

나는 더위를 견딜 수 없어요.

d e n r e u

I can't ________ the heat.

D Choose and complete the sentences.

mistake problem group

1 나는 스터디 그룹을 만들었어요.

I made a study ________.

2 나는 큰 실수를 했어요.

I made a big ________.

3 나는 이 문제를 해결할 수 없어요.

I can't solve this ________.

Day 18 Clothing & Accessories

Check Up Read and check the words you don't know.

1차 복습

- [ ] age
- [ ] problem
- [ ] group
- [ ] noise
- [ ] guy
- [ ] mistake
- [ ] disturb
- [ ] endure

2차 복습

- [ ] road
- [ ] bicycle
- [ ] scare
- [ ] avoid

3차 복습

- [ ] pay
- [ ] coin
- [ ] sale
- [ ] bargain

※망각 제로! 1일 전 3일 전 7일 전 학습한 단어를 복습해요.

Word Tip

age 나이
guy 남자, 사람
road 도로, 길
pay 지불하다, 내다
problem 문제
mistake 실수, 잘못, 오해하다
bicycle 자전거
coin 동전
group 그룹, 무리, 집단
disturb 방해하다
scare 겁주다, 겁먹다
sale 판매
noise 소리, 소음
endure 견디다, 참다
avoid 피하다
bargain 할인한 물건, 흥정

We buy used items.

Pop Quiz Choose and check the right words.

Kiara asks Sally what she thinks of the watch.

키아라는 샐리에게 ____________에 대해 어떻게 생각하는지 물어요.

- [ ] 손목시계
- [ ] 안경

Dennis bought shoes for his sister.

데니스는 여동생을 위한 ____________을 샀어요.

- [ ] 신발
- [ ] 가죽

Catch Up

Listen & Say **Listen, say, and color.**

Read & Write **Write the Basic Words and Jump Up Words.**

watch 손목시계	**The watch is expensive.** 그 손목시계는 비싸요.	n 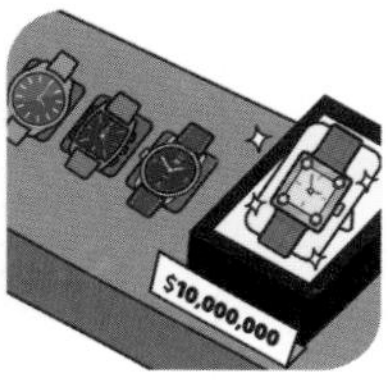
glasses 안경	**These glasses are cheap.** 그 안경은 싸요.	n 
boots 부츠, 목이 긴 신발	**She is wearing boots.** 그녀는 부츠를 신고 있어요.	n 

shoes
신발

n

Shoes protect your feet.

신발은 당신의 발을 보호해요.

borrow
빌리다

v

Can I borrow your coat?

당신의 코트 좀 빌릴 수 있을까요?

ruin
망치다

v

Don't ruin your clothes.

당신의 옷을 망치지 마세요.

hide
숨기다

v

My sister likes to hide my shoes.

내 여동생은 내 신발을 숨기는 것을 좋아해요.

leather
가죽

n

This jacket is made of leather.

이 재킷은 가죽으로 만들어졌어요.

Skill UP

A Find, circle, and write the words.

1 
손목시계
z w a t c h k p

2 
신발
b s h o e s e k

3 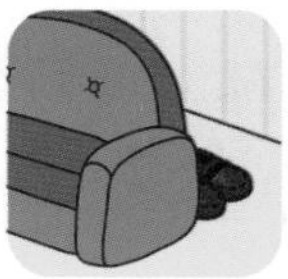
숨기다
k h i d e q x p

4 
망치다
t r u i n e r g

B Choose and write the words.

borrow leather boots glasses

1 안경

2 가죽

3 빌리다

4 부츠, 목이 긴 신발

C Connect and fill in the blanks.

1 

These glasses are cheap.

그 ______________은 싸요.

2 

This jacket is made of leather.

이 재킷은 ______________으로 만들어졌어요.

3 

She is wearing boots.

그녀는 ______________를 신고 있어요.

D Rearrange and write the sentences.

1 신발은 당신의 발을 보호해요.

your | Shoes | feet | protect | .

____

2 당신의 코트 좀 빌릴 수 있을까요?

Can | borrow | your | I | coat | ?

____

Day 19

Cooking

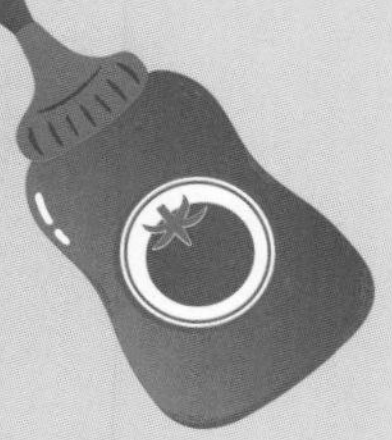

Check Up Read and check the words you don't know.

1차 복습

- [ ] watch
- [ ] glasses
- [ ] boots
- [ ] shoes
- [ ] borrow
- [ ] ruin
- [ ] hide
- [ ] leather

2차 복습

- [ ] king
- [ ] queen
- [ ] coast
- [ ] locate

3차 복습

- [ ] parents
- [ ] friend
- [ ] birthday
- [ ] tradition

※망각 제로! 1일 전 3일 전 7일 전 학습한 단어를 복습해요.

Word Tip

watch 손목시계
borrow 빌리다
king 왕
parents 부모님
glasses 안경
ruin 망치다
queen 여왕
friend 친구
boots 부츠, 목이 긴 신발
hide 숨기다
coast 해안
birthday 생일
shoes 신발
leather 가죽
locate (특정 위치에) 두다
tradition 전통

It smells delicious!

Pop Quiz Choose and check the right words.

Rod's mom tells him to add some salt.

로드의 엄마는 그에게 ____________ 을 좀 넣어 달라고 말해요.

☐ 설탕
☐ 소금

Rod says the stew smells delicious.

로드는 스튜에서 ____________ 냄새가 난다고 말해요.

☐ 맛있는
☐ 두꺼운

Catch Up

Listen & Say Listen, say, and color.

Read & Write Write the **Basic Words** and **Jump Up Words.**

salt 소금	n Add some salt to the pot. 냄비에 소금을 조금 넣으세요.

sugar 설탕	n We need sugar. 우리는 설탕이 필요해요.

oil 기름, 오일	n Put some oil in the pan. 팬에 기름을 조금 두르세요.

delicious
맛있는

a

The food is delicious.

그 음식은 맛있어요.

some
약간의, 조금

det

I need some milk.

나는 약간의 우유가 필요해요.

tender
(음식이) 연한

a

The oil makes it tender.

기름은 그것을 연하게 만들어요.

recipe
조리법, 요리법

n

This recipe is popular.

이 요리법은 인기 있어요.

thick
두꺼운

a

There is a thick slice of bread.

두꺼운 빵 한 조각이 있어요.

Skill UP

A Choose and write the words.

sugar salt oil

1. 
기름, 오일

2. 

소금

3. 

설탕

B Choose and write the words.

delicious thick tender recipe

1. 두꺼운
2. 맛있는
3. 조리법, 요리법
4. (음식이) 연한

C Unscramble and complete the sentences.

1

그 음식은 맛있어요.

e l i d c o s u i

The food is ________.

2

두꺼운 빵 한 조각이 있어요.

h i t k c

There is a ________ slice of bread.

3

이 요리법은 인기 있어요.

r e c p e i

This ________ is popular.

D Choose and complete the sentences.

tender salt some

1 나는 약간의 우유가 필요해요.

I need ________ milk.

2 기름은 그것을 연하게 만들어요.

The oil makes it ________.

3 냄비에 소금을 조금 넣으세요.

Add some ________ to the pot.

Day 20 Home & Town

Check Up Read and check the words you don't know.

1차 복습

☐ salt	☐ some
☐ sugar	☐ tender
☐ oil	☐ thick
☐ delicious	☐ recipe

2차 복습

☐ age	☐ disturb
☐ problem	☐ endure

3차 복습

☐ soccer	☐ exercise
☐ athlete	☐ condition

※**망각 제로!** 1일 전 3일 전 7일 전 학습한 단어를 복습해요.

Word Tip

salt 소금	**sugar** 설탕	**oil** 기름, 오일	**delicious** 맛있는
some 약간의, 조금	**tender** (음식이) 연한	**thick** 두꺼운	**recipe** 조리법, 요리법
age 나이	**problem** 문제	**disturb** 방해하다	**endure** 견디다, 참다
soccer 축구	**athlete** 운동선수	**exercise** 운동하다, 운동	**condition** (경기자의) 컨디션, 상태, 조건

Luna is missing!

Pop Quiz Choose and check the right words.

Rod is looking for Luna in the living room.

로드는 ______________ 에서 루나를 찾고 있어요.

☐ 부엌
☐ 거실

Luna is not in his bedroom.

루나는 ______________ 에 없어요.

☐ 침실
☐ 욕실

Catch Up

Listen & Say Listen, say, and color.

Read & Write Write the Basic Words and Jump Up Words.

bathroom
욕실, 화장실

n

My brother is in the bathroom.
내 남동생은 욕실에 있어요.

bedroom
침실

n

My sister is in her bedroom.
내 여동생은 침실에 있어요.

kitchen
부엌

n

My mom is in the kitchen.
우리 엄마는 부엌에 계세요.

living room
거실

n

My dad is in the living room.

우리 아빠는 거실에 계세요.

garden
정원

n

My grandma is in the garden.

우리 할머니는 정원에 계세요.

ideal
완벽한, 이상적인

a

My home is an ideal place.

우리 집은 완벽한 곳이에요.

observe
관찰하다

v

I observe the moon with a telescope.

나는 망원경으로 달을 관찰해요.

merit
장점

n

My neighborhood has many merits.

우리 동네에는 많은 장점이 있어요.

Skill UP

A Choose and write the words.

garden bedroom bathroom

1 

침실

2 

정원

3 

욕실, 화장실

B Cross out, unscramble, and write the words.

1 부엌 c k i h t n o e

2 관찰하다 o v b e s r e p

3 완벽한, 이상적인 b e i d l a

4 장점 e m r x t i

C Connect and fill in the blanks.

1 

2 

3 

My dad is in the living room.
우리 아빠는 ____________에 계세요.

My mom is in the kitchen.
우리 엄마는 ____________에 계세요.

I observe the moon with a telescope.
나는 망원경으로 달을 ____________.

D Rearrange and write the sentences.

1 우리 할머니는 정원에 계세요.

My | the garden | is | grandma | in | .

2 내 남동생은 욕실에 있어요.

the bathroom | brother | My | is | in | .

WORD SEARCH

Find and circle the hidden pictures.
Then write the words.

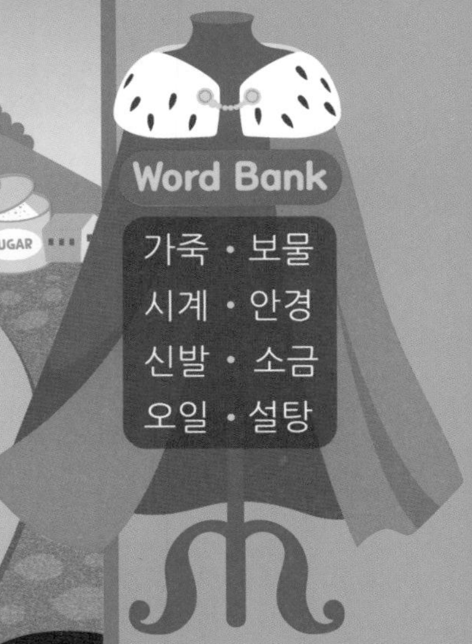

leather

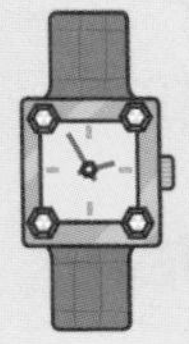

king 왕	queen 여왕	prince 왕자	princess 공주	castle 성

treasure 보물	coast 해안	locate (특정 위치에) 두다	age 나이	problem 문제

group 그룹, 무리, 집단	noise 소리, 소음	guy 남자, 사람	mistake 실수, 잘못, 오해하다	disturb 방해하다

endure 견디다, 참다	watch 손목시계	glasses 안경	boots 부츠, 목이 긴 신발	shoes 신발

borrow 빌리다	ruin 망치다	hide 숨기다	leather 가죽	salt 소금

sugar 설탕	oil 기름, 오일	delicious 맛있는	some 약간의, 조금	tender (음식이) 연한

recipe 조리법, 요리법	thick 두꺼운	bathroom 욕실, 화장실	bedroom 침실	kitchen 부엌

living room 거실	garden 정원	ideal 완벽한, 이상적인	observe 관찰하다	merit 장점

Review TEST

맞힌 개수 : ☐ / 40

① king		㉑ 성	
② queen		㉒ 보물	
③ prince		㉓ 해안	
④ locate		㉔ 공주	
⑤ age		㉕ 남자, 사람	
⑥ mistake		㉖ 문제	
⑦ group		㉗ 방해하다	
⑧ noise		㉘ 견디다, 참다	
⑨ watch		㉙ 빌리다	
⑩ glasses		㉚ 망치다	
⑪ boots		㉛ 숨기다	
⑫ shoes		㉜ 가죽	
⑬ salt		㉝ 약간의, 조금	
⑭ sugar		㉞ (음식이) 연한	
⑮ oil		㉟ 조리법, 요리법	
⑯ delicious		㊱ 두꺼운	
⑰ bathroom		㊲ 정원	
⑱ ideal		㊳ 침실	
⑲ kitchen		㊴ 관찰하다	
⑳ living room		㊵ 장점	

Part 5

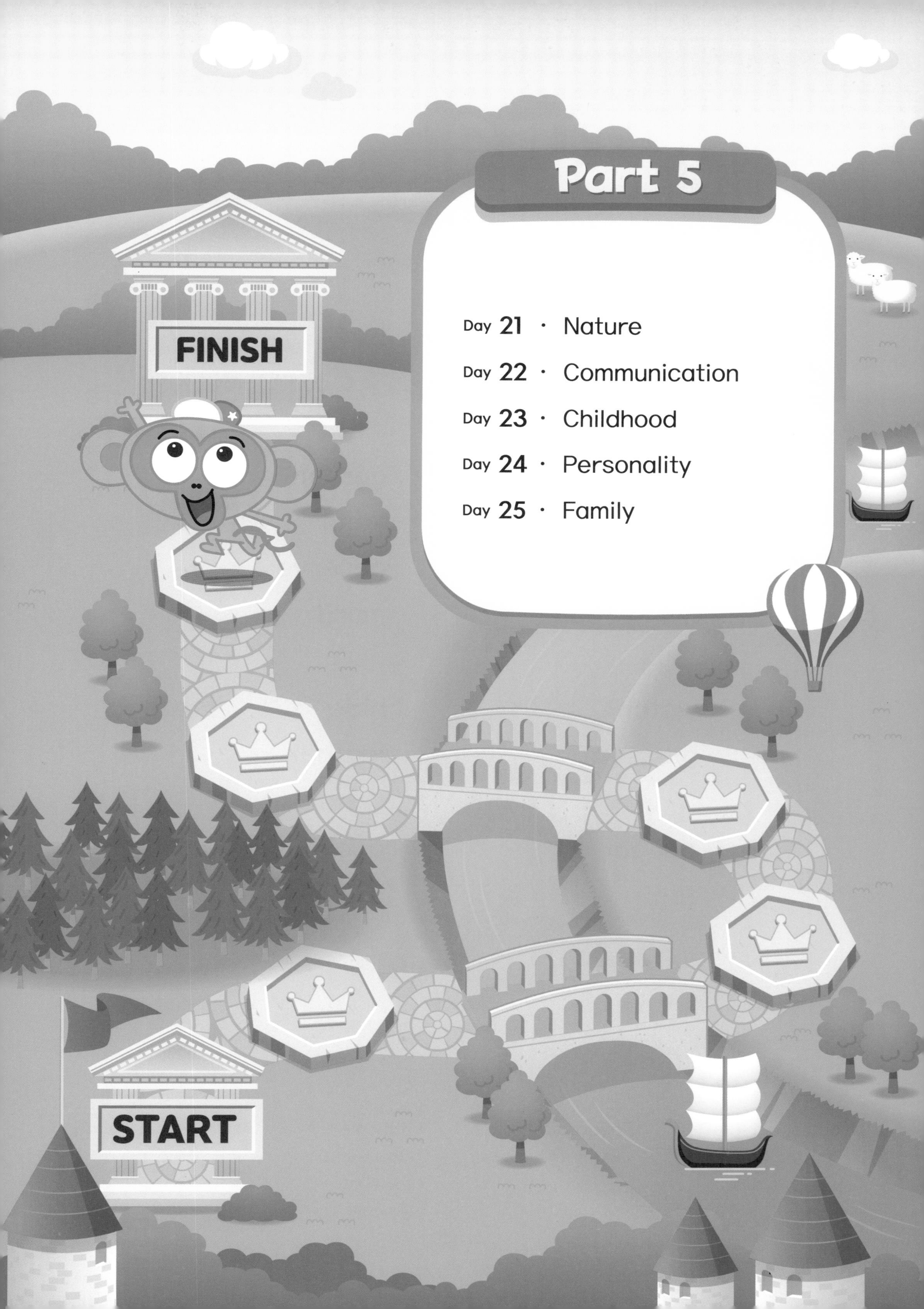

Day 21

Nature

Check Up Read and check the words you don't know.

1차 복습

- [ ] bathroom
- [ ] bedroom
- [ ] kitchen
- [ ] living room
- [ ] garden
- [ ] ideal
- [ ] observe
- [ ] merit

2차 복습

- [ ] watch
- [ ] glasses
- [ ] hide
- [ ] leather

3차 복습

- [ ] danger
- [ ] fog
- [ ] accident
- [ ] prevent

※망각 제로! 1일 전 3일 전 7일 전 학습한 단어를 복습해요.

Word Tip

bathroom 욕실, 화장실
garden 정원
watch 손목시계
danger 위험
bedroom 침실
ideal 완벽한, 이상적인
glasses 안경
fog 안개
kitchen 부엌
observe 관찰하다
hide 숨기다
accident 사고
living room 거실
merit 장점
leather 가죽
prevent 예방하다, 막다

How was your vacation?

Pop Quiz Choose and check the right words.

The teacher asks how they spent their vacation.

선생님이 그들에게 ____________을 어떻게 보냈는지 물어요.

☐ 호수

☐ 방학

Kiara played with sand on the beach.

키아라는 해변에서 ____________를 가지고 놀았어요.

☐ 모래

☐ 잔디

Catch Up

Listen & Say Listen, say, and color.

Read & Write Write the **Basic Words** and **Jump Up Words.**

grass
잔디

n

We lie on the grass.
우리는 잔디 위에 누워요.

stone
돌

n

I collect stones.
나는 돌을 모아요.

sand
모래

n

They play in the sand.
그들은 모래에서 놀아요.

hill
언덕

n

He climbs the hill.

그가 언덕에 올라요.

lake
호수

n

Some ducks are on the lake.

오리 몇 마리가 호수에 있어요.

vacation
방학, 휴가

n

I went camping during the vacation.

나는 방학 동안 캠핑을 하러 갔어요.

exhausted
기진맥진한

a

The students are exhausted after hiking.

학생들은 하이킹 후에 기진맥진해 있어요.

remote
외딴, 먼

a

This remote place is calm.

이 외딴 곳은 조용해요.

Skill UP

A Find, circle, and write the words.

❶ 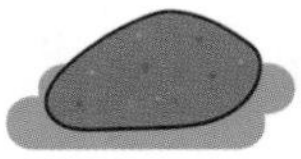

y s t o n e w g

돌

❷ 

p s h i l l e k

언덕

❸ 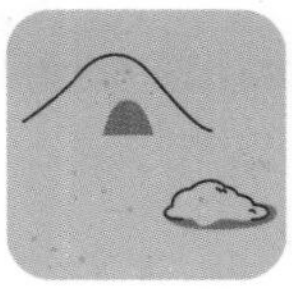

u w o h s a n d

모래

❹ 

q l a k e m r t

호수

B Choose and write the words.

exhausted	remote	vacation	grass

❶ 외딴, 먼

❷ 방학, 휴가

❸ 잔디

❹ 기진맥진한

C Unscramble and complete the sentences.

1 

c o v a a n i t

나는 방학 동안 캠핑을 하러 갔어요.

I went camping during the ________.

2 

m e r e t o

이 외딴 곳은 조용해요.

This ________ place is calm.

3 

s s a g r

우리는 잔디 위에 누워요.

We lie on the ________.

D Choose and complete the sentences.

hill lake sand

1 그들은 모래에서 놀아요.

They play in the ________.

2 오리 몇 마리가 호수에 있어요.

Some ducks are on the ________.

3 그가 언덕에 올라요.

He climbs the ________.

Day 22

Communication

Check Up Read and check the words you don't know.

1차 복습

- [ ] grass
- [ ] stone
- [ ] sand
- [ ] hill
- [ ] lake
- [ ] vacation
- [ ] exhausted
- [ ] remote

2차 복습

- [ ] salt
- [ ] sugar
- [ ] recipe
- [ ] thick

3차 복습

- [ ] prince
- [ ] princess
- [ ] castle
- [ ] treasure

※망각 제로! 1일 전 3일 전 7일 전 학습한 단어를 복습해요.

Word Tip

grass 잔디	stone 돌	sand 모래	hill 언덕
lake 호수	vacation 방학, 휴가	exhausted 기진맥진한	remote 외딴, 먼
salt 소금	sugar 설탕	recipe 조리법, 요리법	thick 두꺼운
prince 왕자	princess 공주	castle 성	treasure 보물

Do you need my help?

Pop Quiz Choose and check the right words.

Dennis asks his parents if they need help.

데니스는 부모님에게 도움이 ____________지 물어요.

☐ 필요하다
☐ 선택하다

Dennis's dad thinks they're fortunate to have a nice son.

데니스의 아빠는 착한 아들이 있어서 ____________다고 생각해요.

☐ 운 좋은
☐ 전달하다

Catch UP

Listen & Say Listen, say, and color.

Read & Write Write the **Basic Words** and **Jump Up Words.**

understand
이해하다

I can understand.
나는 이해할 수 있어요.

need
필요하다

I need to talk to a friend.
나는 친구와 대화가 필요해요.

choose
선택하다

I choose words carefully.
나는 단어를 신중하게 선택해요.

carry
전달하다, 나르다

v

They carry a message for the king.
그들은 왕에게 메시지를 전달해요.

miss
그리워하다, 놓치다

v

I miss my friend.
나는 내 친구가 그리워요.

fortunate
운 좋은

a

I'm fortunate to have a big family.
나는 대가족이라 운이 좋아요.

environment
환경

n

A friendly environment is good for communication.
친화적인 환경은 의사소통에 좋아요.

emotion
감정

n

I can feel your emotions.
나는 당신의 감정들을 느낄 수 있어요.

Skill UP

A Choose and write the words.

emotion　　miss　　carry

1

전달하다, 나르다

2

그리워하다, 놓치다

3

감정

B Choose and write the words.

choose　　environment　　need　　understand

1 이해하다

2 환경

3 선택하다

4 필요하다

C Connect and fill in the blanks.

1 

2 

3 

I'm fortunate to have a big family.

나는 대가족이라 ______________ 요.

I can understand.

나는 ___________ 수 있어요.

I choose words carefully.

나는 단어를 신중하게 ___________.

D Rearrange and write the sentences.

1 나는 당신의 감정들을 느낄 수 있어요.

I feel can emotions your .

2 나는 내 친구가 그리워요.

my friend miss I .

Day 23

Childhood

Check Up Read and check the words you don't know.

1차 복습

- [ ] understand
- [ ] need
- [ ] choose
- [ ] carry
- [ ] miss
- [ ] fortunate
- [ ] environment
- [ ] emotion

2차 복습

- [ ] bathroom
- [ ] bedroom
- [ ] observe
- [ ] merit

3차 복습

- [ ] group
- [ ] noise
- [ ] guy
- [ ] mistake

※망각 제로! 1일 전 3일 전 7일 전 학습한 단어를 복습해요.

Word Tip

understand 이해하다	need 필요하다	choose 선택하다	carry 전달하다, 나르다
miss 그리워하다, 놓치다	fortunate 운 좋은	environment 환경	emotion 감정
bathroom 욕실, 화장실	bedroom 침실	observe 관찰하다	merit 장점
group 그룹, 무리, 집단	noise 소리, 소음	guy 남자, 사람	mistake 실수, 잘못, 오해하다

Is this Lily or Dennis?

Pop Quiz Choose and check the right words.

Baby Dennis is crying in the picture.

사진 속 아기 데니스는 __________ 있어요.

☐ 돌보다
☐ 울다

Lily always clings to her mom.

릴리는 항상 엄마에게 __________.

☐ 매달리다
☐ 이해하다

Catch Up

Listen & Say Listen, say, and color.

Read & Write Write the Basic Words and Jump Up Words.

child
아이, 어린이

n

A child is reading a book.
한 아이가 책을 읽고 있어요.

adult
어른, 성인

n

He is an adult.
그는 어른이에요.

care
돌보다, 돌봄, 보살핌

v n

She cares for her sick children.
그녀는 아픈 자녀들을 돌봐요.

birth
탄생, 출생

n

We celebrated the birth of my baby.

우리는 내 아기의 탄생을 축하했어요.

cry
울다

v

Does she cry in the night?

그녀가 밤중에 우나요?

infant
아기, 유아

n

The infant slept soundly.

그 아기는 푹 잤어요.

cling
매달리다, 달라붙다

v

The children cling to their mother.

아이들이 엄마에게 매달려요.

monster
괴물

n

The child was afraid of the monster.

그 아이는 괴물을 무서워했어요.

Skill UP

A Find, circle, and write the words.

1

아이, 어린이

s c h i l d w y

2

어른, 성인

s h a d u l t k

3

탄생, 출생

u b i r t h q p d

4

괴물

n m o n s t e r

B Cross out, unscramble, and write the words.

1. 돌보다, 돌봄, 보살핌 — r m c e a
2. 울다 — c k y r
3. 매달리다, 달라붙다 — c i g a l n
4. 아기, 유아 — f a e n t i n

C Connect and fill in the blanks.

1  • • The children cling to their mother.

아이들이 엄마에게 ___________.

2  • • The infant slept soundly.

그 ___________는 푹 잤어요.

3  • • Does she cry in the night?

그녀가 밤중에 ___________?

D Choose and complete the sentences.

cares birth child

1 그녀는 아픈 자녀들을 돌봐요.

She ___________ for her sick children.

2 한 아이가 책을 읽고 있어요.

A ___________ is reading a book.

3 우리는 내 아기의 탄생을 축하했어요.

We celebrated the ___________ of my baby.

Day 24 Personality

Check Up Read and check the words you don't know.

1차 복습

- [ ] child
- [ ] adult
- [ ] care
- [ ] birth
- [ ] cry
- [ ] infant
- [ ] cling
- [ ] monster

2차 복습

- [ ] grass
- [ ] stone
- [ ] exhausted
- [ ] remote

3차 복습

- [ ] boots
- [ ] shoes
- [ ] borrow
- [ ] ruin

※망각 제로! 1일 전 3일 전 7일 전 학습한 단어를 복습해요.

Word Tip

child 아이, 어린이
cry 울다
grass 잔디
boots 부츠, 목이 긴 신발
adult 어른, 성인
infant 아기, 유아
stone 돌
shoes 신발
care 돌보다, 돌봄, 보살핌
cling 매달리다, 달라붙다
exhausted 기진맥진한
borrow 빌리다
birth 탄생, 출생
monster 괴물
remote 외딴, 먼
ruin 망치다

Tom is very shy.

Pop Quiz Choose and check the right words.

Kiara thinks Sally looks upset.

키아라는 샐리가 ____________ 보인다고 생각해요.

☐ 속상한
☐ 게으른

Kiara says Tom is just shy.

키아라는 톰이 그냥 ____________ 거라고 말해요.

☐ 수줍어하는
☐ 사회적인

Catch UP

Listen & Say

Listen, say, and color.

Read & Write

Write the **Basic Words** and **Jump Up Words**.

glad
기쁜

a

I am glad to see you.
나는 당신을 만나서 기뻐요.

upset
화난, 속상한

a

She is upset.
그녀는 화가 났어요.

crazy
정상이 아닌,
미친

a

He is crazy.
그는 정상이 아니에요.

lazy
게으른

a

She was feeling lazy.

그녀는 게으르다고 느꼈어요.

shy
수줍어하는

a

The girl is shy.

그 여자아이는 수줍어해요.

stable
안정된, 차분한

a

She is emotionally stable.

그녀는 정서적으로 안정되어 있어요.

wit
재치, 기지

n

She showed off her wit.

그녀는 재치를 뽐냈어요.

social
사교적인, 사회적인

a

He is a social person.

그는 사교적인 사람이에요.

Skill UP

A Choose and write the words.

shy glad crazy

1. 

기쁜

2. 

정상이 아닌, 미친

3. 

수줍어하는

B Cross out, unscramble, and write the words.

1. 안정된, 차분한 — t e s a l b u
2. 화난, 속상한 — u d p e t s
3. 사교적인, 사회적인 — t c i s a l o
4. 재치, 기지 — w r i t

C Unscramble and complete the sentences.

1 

그녀는 게으르다고 느꼈어요.

zlay

She was feeling ________.

2 

그녀는 화가 났어요.

eupst

She is ________.

3 

그녀는 재치를 뽐냈어요.

tiw

She showed off her ________.

D Rearrange and write the sentences.

1 나는 당신을 만나서 기뻐요.

I | glad | you | am | to | see | .

2 그 여자아이는 수줍어해요.

is | The | girl | shy | .

Day 25

Family

Check Up Read and check the words you don't know.

1차 복습

- [ ] glad
- [ ] upset
- [ ] crazy
- [ ] lazy
- [ ] shy
- [ ] stable
- [ ] wit
- [ ] social

2차 복습

- [ ] understand
- [ ] need
- [ ] environment
- [ ] emotion

3차 복습

- [ ] oil
- [ ] delicious
- [ ] some
- [ ] tender

※망각 제로! 1일 전 3일 전 7일 전 학습한 단어를 복습해요.

Word Tip

glad 기쁜	upset 화난, 속상한	crazy 정상이 아닌, 미친	lazy 게으른
shy 수줍어하는	stable 안정된, 차분한	wit 재치, 기지	social 사교적인, 사회적인
understand 이해하다	need 필요하다	environment 환경	emotion 감정
oil 기름, 오일	delicious 맛있는	some 약간의, 조금	tender (음식이) 연한

Let's take a video of our family.

Pop Quiz Choose and check the right words.

Rod's dad introduces his lovely wife.

로드의 아빠는 사랑스러운 ______________ 를 소개해요.

☐ 남편
☐ 아내

Their children are watching TV together.

아이들은 ______________ TV를 보고 있어요.

☐ 주요한
☐ 함께

Catch Up

Listen & Say Listen, say, and color.

Read & Write Write the **Basic Words** and **Jump Up Words.**

husband
남편

n

He is my husband.
그는 내 남편이에요.

wife
아내, 부인

n

She is my wife.
그녀는 내 아내예요.

daughter
딸

n

Her daughter is cute.
그녀의 딸은 귀여워요.

son
아들

n

His son is handsome.

그의 아들은 잘생겼어요.

together
함께

adv

We have dinner together.

우리는 함께 저녁을 먹어요.

major
중요한, 중대한

a

She plays a major role in our family.

그녀는 우리 가족에서 중요한 역할을 해요.

stamp
우표, 도장

n

I need a stamp for this letter.

나는 이 편지에 붙일 우표가 필요해요.

ambition
야망, 포부

n

He has one ambition in life.

그는 인생에 한 가지 야망이 있어요.

Skill UP

A Choose and write the words.

wife husband son

1 

아내, 부인

2 

아들

3 

남편

B Choose and write the words.

daughter major ambition together

1 중요한, 중대한

2 함께

3 딸

4 야망, 포부

C Connect and fill in the blanks.

① 

② 

③ 

Her daughter is cute.
그녀의 ____________은 귀여워요.

I need a stamp for this letter.
나는 이 편지에 붙일 ____________가 필요해요.

We have dinner together.
우리는 ____________ 저녁을 먹어요.

D Rearrange and write the sentences.

① 그의 아들은 잘생겼어요.

His | is | son | handsome | .

② 그는 인생에 한 가지 야망이 있어요.

has | ambition | one | He | life | in | .

WORD PUZZLE Complete the word puzzle.

ACROSS

② The girl is ________.

③ He is an ________.

⑤ They ________ a message for the king.

⑦ I ________ my friend.

⑧ I collect ________s.

DOWN

① He is ________.

② I need a ________ for this letter.

④ We lie on the ________.

⑤ A ________ is reading a book.

⑥ She is my ________.

Day 21~25

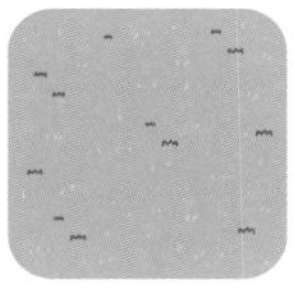 **grass** 잔디	 **stone** 돌	 **sand** 모래	 **hill** 언덕	 **lake** 호수
 **vacation** 방학, 휴가	 **exhausted** 기진맥진한	 **remote** 외딴, 먼	 **understand** 이해하다	 **need** 필요하다
 **choose** 선택하다	 **carry** 전달하다, 나르다	 **miss** 그리워하다, 놓치다	 **fortunate** 운 좋은	 **environment** 환경
 **emotion** 감정	 **child** 아이, 어린이	 **adult** 어른, 성인	 **care** 돌보다, 돌봄, 보살핌	 **birth** 탄생, 출생
 **cry** 울다	 **infant** 아기, 유아	 **cling** 매달리다, 달라붙다	 **monster** 괴물	 **glad** 기쁜
 **upset** 화난, 속상한	 **crazy** 정상이 아닌, 미친	 **lazy** 게으른	 **shy** 수줍어하는	 **stable** 안정된, 차분한
 **wit** 재치, 기지	 **social** 사교적인, 사회적인	 **husband** 남편	 **wife** 아내, 부인	 **daughter** 딸
 **son** 아들	 **together** 함께	 **major** 중요한, 중대한	 **stamp** 우표, 도장	 **ambition** 야망, 포부

Review TEST

맞힌 개수 : ☐ / 40

1 grass		21 호수	
2 stone		22 방학, 휴가	
3 sand		23 기진맥진한	
4 hill		24 외딴, 먼	
5 miss		25 이해하다	
6 need		26 운 좋은	
7 choose		27 환경	
8 carry		28 감정	
9 child		29 울다	
10 adult		30 아기, 유아	
11 care		31 탄생, 출생	
12 cling		32 괴물	
13 glad		33 수줍어하는	
14 upset		34 안정된, 차분한	
15 crazy		35 재치, 기지	
16 social		36 게으른	
17 husband		37 함께	
18 wife		38 중요한, 중대한	
19 daughter		39 우표, 도장	
20 son		40 야망, 포부	

Answer Key

Level 2.1

Day 01

P11

Pop Quiz ☑ 곰 ☐ 코끼리 ☑ 얼룩말 ☐ 원숭이

P14~15

Skill up

A Choose and write the words.

monkey bear zebra

1. bear 곰
2. monkey 원숭이
3. zebra 얼룩말

B Cross out, unscramble, and write the words.

1. 코끼리 pelmeatnh — elephant
2. 원숭이 nkxomye — monkey
3. 달아나다, 탈출하다 sxceaep — escape
4. 동물 xnamlia — animal

C Connect and fill in the blanks.

1. A mouse found a hole. 쥐가 구멍 을 발견했어요.
2. An elephant is in the water. 코끼리 가 물속에 있어요.
3. We trace a tiger's paw prints. 우리는 호랑이의 발자국을 추적해요 .

D Rearrange and write the sentences.

1. 얼룩말이 달리고 있어요. running / A zebra / is / .
A zebra is running.
2. 곰이 동굴 안에 있어요. A bear / is / the cave / in / .
A bear is in the cave.

14 15

Day 02

P17

Pop Quiz ☑ 허리 ☐ 무릎 ☐ 약 ☑ 병원

P20~21

Skill up

A Find, circle, and write the words.

1. 손가락 mfingern — finger
2. 무릎 saknee o — knee
3. 허리, 등 kdbackt — back
4. 턱 rfsching — chin

B Choose and write the words.

toe hospital examine drug

1. 발가락 toe toe
2. 병원 hospital hospital
3. 약 drug drug
4. 진찰하다, 조사하다 examine examine

C Unscramble and complete the sentences.

1. 병원에는 많은 의사들이 있어요. pihsoalt
A hospital has many doctors.
2. 의사가 당신을 진찰할 거예요. eamiexn
The doctor will examine you.
3. 이 약은 환자의 회복을 도와요. rudg
This drug helps patients recover.

D Choose and complete the sentences.

knee toes finger

1. 내 발가락이 아주 아파요.
My toes hurt a lot.
2. 아픈 무릎에는 휴식이 필요해요.
A sore knee needs rest.
3. 그의 손가락은 길어요.
His finger is long.

20 21

Day 03

P23

Pop Quiz ☐ 미술 ☑ 수학 ☑ 재능 ☐ 과목

P26~27

Skill Up

A Choose and write the words.

math science art

❶  math 수학

❷  art 미술

❸  science 과학

B Choose and write the words.

subject favorite solve music

❶ 음악	music	music
❷ 과목, 주제	subject	subject
❸ 풀다, 해결하다	solve	solve
❹ 매우 좋아하는	favorite	favorite

26

C Unscramble and complete the sentences.

❶  그녀는 다양한 재능을 가지고 있어요. antelts
She has different talents .

❷  퍼즐을 풀자. osvel
Let's solve the puzzle.

❸  당신이 가장 좋아하는 과목이 무엇인가요? usbcejt
What is your favorite subject ?

D Rearrange and write the sentences.

❶ 그는 과학을 좋아해요.
likes He science .
He likes science.

❷ 우리는 수학 시간에 도형을 배우고 있어요.
math class are learning in shapes We .
We are learning shapes in math class.

27

Day 04

P29

Pop Quiz ☑ 전문가 ☐ 말하다 ☑ 대답하다 ☐ 초대하다

P32~33

Skill Up

A Choose and write the words.

ask invite speak

❶  speak 말하다

❷  invite 초대하다

❸  ask 묻다

B Cross out, unscramble, and write the words.

❶ 대답하다	sanewxr	answer
❷ 전체의, 온	ntgeier	entire
❸ 전문가	epxetrx	expert
❹ 궁금해하다	xwnerdo	wonder

32

C Connect and fill in the blanks.

❶ 

❷ 

❸ 

I wonder what my friend will say.
나는 내 친구가 뭐라고 말할지 궁금해요 .

She is a public speaking expert.
그녀는 연설 전문가 예요.

We listen to music.
우리는 음악을 들어요 .

D Choose and complete the sentences.

entire invite speak

❶ 그들은 나를 파티에 초대해요.
They invite me to the party.

❷ 나는 전체 이야기를 듣고 싶어요.
I want to hear the entire story.

❸ 나는 영어로 말할 수 있어요.
I can speak English.

33

Day 05

P35

Pop Quiz ☐ 배부른 ☑ 배고픈 ☐ 맛이 쓴 ☑ 달콤한

P38~39

Skill Up

A Find, circle, and write the words.

1. 달콤한 csweetd — sweet
2. 배부른 shfully — full
3. 굽다 hdbakek — bake
4. 밀봉하다 rfsealkq — seal

B Choose and write the words.

advise bitter tea hungry

1. 배고픈 — hungry hungry
2. 맛이 쓴, 격렬한 — bitter bitter
3. 차, 찻잎 — seal seal
4. 충고하다 — advise advise

38

C Unscramble and complete the sentences.

1. 나는 배가 고파요. uhnyrg
I'm feeling hungry .
2. 나는 차 마시는 것을 좋아해요. aet
I like drinking tea .
3. 그 커피는 맛이 썼어요. ibttre
The coffee tasted bitter .

D Rearrange and write the sentences.

1. 나는 피자를 먹어서 배불러요.
full I'm pizza eating after .
I'm full after eating pizza.
2. 나는 달콤한 과일을 먹는 것을 아주 좋아해요.
love I eating fruit sweet .
I love eating sweet fruit.

39

Day 01~05

P40

Word Maze Follow the correctly spelled words.

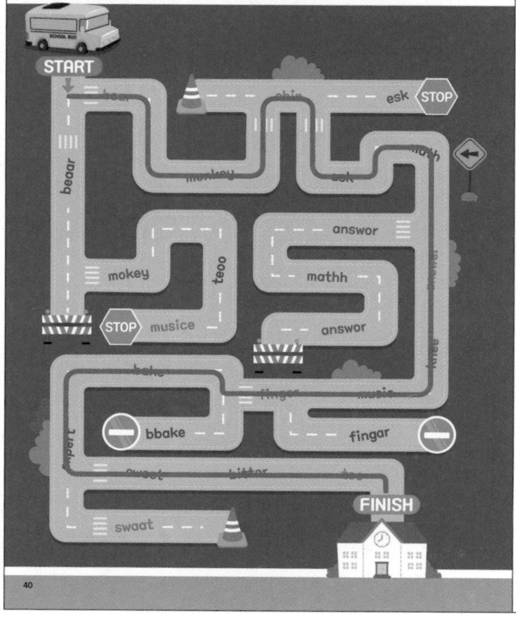

40

P42

Review Test

맞힌 개수 : /40

1 animal	동물	21 얼룩말	zebra
2 bear	곰	22 코끼리	elephant
3 escape	달아나다, 탈출하다	23 추적하다, 흔적	trace
4 monkey	원숭이	24 구멍	hole
5 finger	손가락	25 약	drug
6 back	허리, 등	26 발가락	toe
7 knee	무릎	27 병원	hospital
8 examine	진찰하다, 조사하다	28 턱	chin
9 art	미술	29 과목, 주제	subject
10 math	수학	30 풀다, 해결하다	solve
11 science	과학	31 재능, 재주	talent
12 music	음악	32 매우 좋아하는	favorite
13 answer	대답하다	33 듣다	listen
14 ask	묻다	34 전체의, 온	entire
15 speak	말하다	35 전문가	expert
16 invite	초대하다	36 궁금해하다	wonder
17 sweet	달콤한	37 굽다	bake
18 full	배부른	38 밀봉하다	seal
19 hungry	배고픈	39 맛이 쓴, 격렬한	bitter
20 advise	충고하다	40 차, 찻잎	tea

42

Day 06

P45

Pop Quiz ☑ 바닥 ☐ 창문 ☐ 문 ☑ 벽

P48~49

Skill Up

A Choose and write the words.

floor window passage

1 window 창문
2 floor 바닥, 층
3 passage 통로, 복도

B Cross out, unscramble, and write the words.

1 계단 srxasit — stairs
2 문 rxodo — door
3 벽 awllx — wall
4 실제의 aucalxt — actual

C Connect and fill in the blanks.

1 He hung a picture on the wall.
그는 벽 에 그림을 걸었어요.

2 The dog likes to sit on the stairs.
그 개는 계단 에 앉는 것을 좋아해요.

3 Knock on the door first.
문 을 먼저 두드리세요.

D Choose and complete the sentences.

actual window floor

1 바닥이 차가워요.
The floor is cold.

2 그 방의 실제 크기는 커요.
The actual size of the room is big.

3 고양이가 창문 밖을 내다보고 있어요.
The cat is looking out the window.

Day 07

P51

Pop Quiz ☐ 겨울 ☑ 봄 ☑ 여름 ☐ 가을

P54~55

Skill Up

A Find, circle, and write the words.

1 c(spring)d — spring 봄
2 k(summer)r — summer 여름
3 kd(fall)ee — fall 가을
4 (winter)yz — winter 겨울

B Choose and write the words.

mild chill climate season

1 냉기, 오한 chill chill
2 온화한, 순한 mild mild
3 계절 season season
4 기후 climate climate

C Unscramble and complete the sentences.

1 나는 공기에서 차가움을 느껴요. hclil
I feel a chill in the air.

2 오늘은 날씨가 온화해요. idlm
The weather is mild today.

3 한국에는 사계절이 있어요. saoenss
There are four seasons in Korea.

D Rearrange and write the sentences.

1 그녀는 봄을 즐기고 있어요.
spring She is enjoying .
She is enjoying spring.

2 우리는 겨울에 눈사람을 만들어요.
make We a snowman winter in .
We make a snowman in winter.

Day 08

P57

Pop Quiz ☑ 기억하다 ☐ 허락하다 ☐ 받다 ☑ 주다

P60~61

Skill up

A Choose and write the words.

give get remember

❶	❷	❸
get	remember	give
받다, 구하다	기억하다	주다

B Choose and write the words.

feel experience allow precious

❶	느끼다	feel	feel
❷	경험	experience	experience
❸	소중한, 귀중한	precious	precious
❹	허락하다	allow	allow

C Connect and fill in the blanks.

❶ I feel happy when I play.
나는 놀 때 행복을 느껴요.

❷ He sends an email.
그는 이메일을 보내요.

❸ My toy is precious to me.
내 장난감은 나에게 소중해 요.

D Choose and complete the sentences.

experience give allow

❶ 엄마에게 선물을 드리자.
Let's give gifts to Mom.

❷ 엄마는 우리가 여행하는 것을 허락할 거예요.
Mom will allow us to go on a trip.

❸ 자전거를 타는 것은 재미있는 경험이에요.
Riding a bike is a fun experience.

Day 09

P63

Pop Quiz ☑ 영리한 ☐ 못생긴 ☐ 뚱뚱한 ☑ 우아한

P66~67

Skill up

A Choose and write the words.

ugly loyal clever

❶	❷	❸
clever	ugly	loyal
영리한	못생긴	충성스러운

B Cross out, unscramble, and write the words.

❶ 침착한, 차분한	x l a m c	calm
❷ 아름다운	b a e f l t i u x u	beautiful
❸ 뛰어난, 훌륭한	b l l i n r x a t i	brilliant
❹ 우아한	l e g a x e n t	elegant

C Connect and fill in the blanks.

A pig is fat.
돼지는 뚱뚱해 요.

The ballerina is very elegant.
발레리나는 매우 우아해 요.

The flowers are beautiful.
꽃이 아름다워 요.

D Rearrange and write the sentences.

❶ 우리 아빠는 항상 침착해요.
calm / My / is always / dad / .
My dad is always calm.

❷ 내 남동생은 영리해요.
brother / My / little / clever / is / .
My little brother is clever.

Day 10

P69

Pop Quiz ☑ 강한 ☐ 약한 ☑ 똑똑한 ☐ 따분한

P72~73

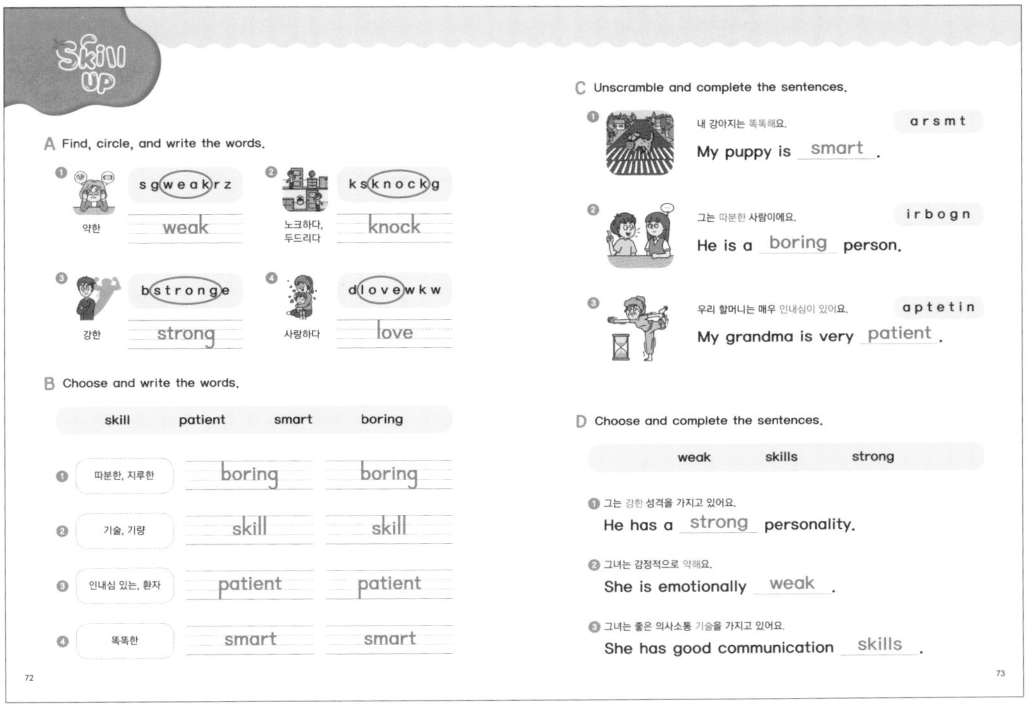
Skill Up

A Find, circle, and write the words.

❶ 약한	s g (w e a k) r z	weak
❷ 노크하다, 두드리다	k s (k n o c k) g	knock
❸ 강한	b (s t r o n g) e	strong
❹ 사랑하다	d (l o v e) w k w	love

B Choose and write the words.

skill patient smart boring

❶ 따분한, 지루한	boring	boring
❷ 기술, 기량	skill	skill
❸ 인내심 있는, 환자	patient	patient
❹ 똑똑한	smart	smart

72

C Unscramble and complete the sentences.

❶ 내 강아지는 똑똑해요. arsmt
My puppy is smart.

❷ 그는 따분한 사람이에요. irbogn
He is a boring person.

❸ 우리 할머니는 매우 인내심이 있어요. aptetin
My grandma is very patient.

D Choose and complete the sentences.

weak skills strong

❶ 그는 강한 성격을 가지고 있어요.
He has a strong personality.

❷ 그녀는 감정적으로 약해요.
She is emotionally weak.

❸ 그녀는 좋은 의사소통 기술을 가지고 있어요.
She has good communication skills.

73

Day 06~10

P74

Word Search Find, circle, and write the words.

Words go in 2 directions→↓

w	e	c	h	i	l	l	f	a	h
i	d	o	o	r	l	t	e	g	g
n	k	b	t	t	c	s	e	y	i
t	e	r	c	l	l	t	l	x	v
e	l	w	u	o	e	r	v	x	e
r	e	a	i	v	v	o	l	b	n
e	g	l	u	e	e	n	i	a	z
b	a	l	e	u	r	g	u	n	z
q	n	i	g	y	d	g	f	w	u
i	t	k	w	z	z	c	e	x	n

Word Bank: door, wall, clever, chill, feel, give, winter, elegant, strong, love

door wall winter chill feel

give clever elegant strong love

74

P76

Review TEST

맞힌 개수 : ☐ / 40

❶ door	문	㉑ 계단	stairs
❷ floor	바닥, 층	㉒ 통로, 복도	passage
❸ wall	벽	㉓ 실제의	actual
❹ window	창문	㉔ 분위기, 대기	atmosphere
❺ spring	봄	㉕ 계절	season
❻ summer	여름	㉖ 냉기, 오한	chill
❼ fall	가을	㉗ 기후	climate
❽ winter	겨울	㉘ 온화한, 순한	mild
❾ feel	느끼다	㉙ 보내다	send
❿ get	받다, 구하다	㉚ 허락하다	allow
⓫ give	주다	㉛ 소중한, 귀중한	precious
⓬ remember	기억하다	㉜ 경험	experience
⓭ beautiful	아름다운	㉝ 영리한	clever
⓮ ugly	못생긴	㉞ 뛰어난, 훌륭한	brilliant
⓯ fat	뚱뚱한	㉟ 우아한	elegant
⓰ calm	침착한, 차분한	㊱ 충성스러운	loyal
⓱ strong	강한	㊲ 똑똑한	smart
⓲ weak	약한	㊳ 기술, 기량	skill
⓳ love	사랑하다	㊴ 노크하다, 두드리다	knock
⓴ boring	따분한, 지루한	㊵ 인내심 있는, 환자	patient

76

Day 11

P79

Pop Quiz ☐ 최고의 ☑ 환상적인 ☑ 천재 ☐ 노래

P82~83

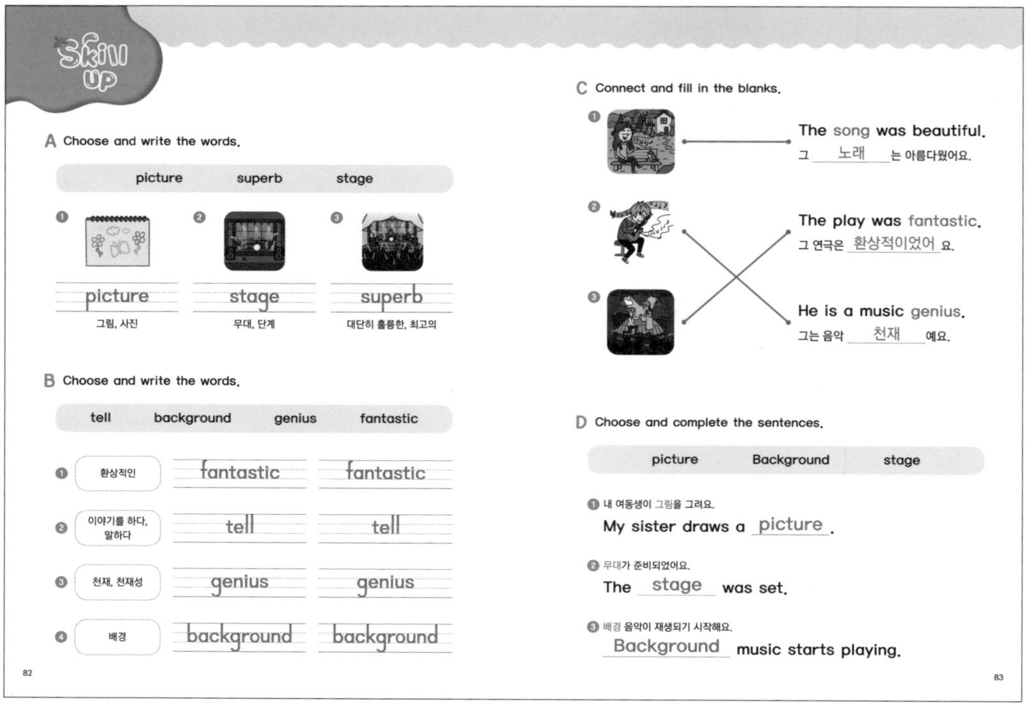

Skill Up

A Choose and write the words.

picture superb stage

1 picture 그림, 사진
2 stage 무대, 단계
3 superb 대단히 훌륭한, 최고의

B Choose and write the words.

tell background genius fantastic

1 환상적인 fantastic fantastic
2 이야기를 하다, 말하다 tell tell
3 천재, 천재성 genius genius
4 배경 background background

C Connect and fill in the blanks.

1 The song was beautiful. 그 노래 는 아름다웠어요.
2 The play was fantastic. 그 연극은 환상적이었어 요.
3 He is a music genius. 그는 음악 천재 예요.

D Choose and complete the sentences.

picture Background stage

1 내 여동생이 그림을 그려요. My sister draws a picture .
2 무대가 준비되었어요. The stage was set.
3 배경 음악이 재생되기 시작해요. Background music starts playing.

82 83

Day 12

P85

Pop Quiz ☑ 판매 ☐ 동전 ☑ 비싼 ☐ 싼

P88~89

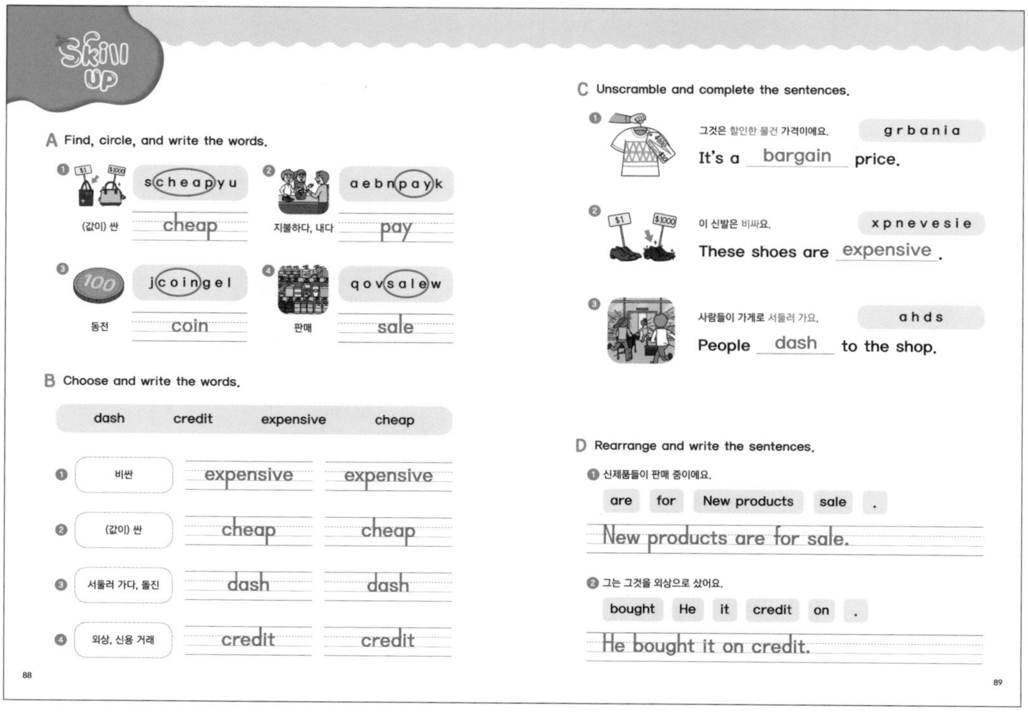

Skill Up

A Find, circle, and write the words.

1 scheapyu (값이) 싼 cheap
2 aebnpayk 지불하다, 내다 pay
3 jcoingel 동전 coin
4 qovsalew 판매 sale

B Choose and write the words.

dash credit expensive cheap

1 비싼 expensive expensive
2 (값이) 싼 cheap cheap
3 서둘러 가다, 돌진 dash dash
4 외상, 신용 거래 credit credit

C Unscramble and complete the sentences.

1 그것은 할인한 물건 가격이에요. grbania It's a bargain price.
2 이 신발은 비싸요. xpnevesie These shoes are expensive .
3 사람들이 가게로 서둘러 가요. ahds People dash to the shop.

D Rearrange and write the sentences.

1 신제품들이 판매 중이에요. are for New products sale .
New products are for sale.
2 그는 그것을 외상으로 샀어요. bought He it credit on .
He bought it on credit.

88 89

Day 13

P91

Pop Quiz ☐ 기념일 ☑ 깜짝 놀라게 하기 ☐ 전통 ☑ 친구

P94~95

Skill up

A Choose and write the words.

friend father parents

❶ father 아버지
❷ friend 친구
❸ parents 부모님

B Cross out, unscramble, and write the words.

❶ 어머니 — kmhroet — mother
❷ 놀라움, 깜짝 놀라게 하기 — saruopersi — surprise
❸ 생일 — dbgaihtyr — birthday
❹ 전통 — titdakorni — tradition

C Connect and fill in the blanks.

❶ Today is my birthday.
오늘은 내 생일 이에요.

❷ Today is our wedding anniversary.
오늘은 우리의 결혼 기념일 이에요.

❸ The party was a big surprise.
그 파티는 큰 놀라움 이었어요.

D Choose and complete the sentences.

mother parents tradition

❶ 우리 어머니는 케이크를 구웠어요.
My mother baked a cake.

❷ 나는 우리 부모님을 사랑해요.
I love my parents .

❸ 우리는 그 전통을 따라요.
We follow that tradition .

94 95

Day 14

P97

Pop Quiz ☐ 야구 ☑ 상태 ☑ 운동하다 ☐ 경쟁하다

P100~101

Skill up

A Find, circle, and write the words.

❶ ehsoccerg — soccer 축구
❷ nbaseball — baseball 야구
❸ eathletef — athlete 운동선수
❹ exerciset — exercise 운동하다, 운동

B Choose and write the words.

defeat basketball condition compete

❶ 이기다, (상대를) 패배시키다 — defeat — defeat
❷ (경기자의) 컨디션, 상태, 조건 — condition — condition
❸ 농구 — basketball — basketball
❹ 경쟁하다, 겨루다 — compete — compete

C Connect and fill in the blanks.

❶ We love playing basketball.
우리는 농구 하는 것을 아주 좋아해요.

❷ The players are in good condition.
그 선수들은 컨디션 이 좋아요.

❸ We compete in tournaments.
우리는 토너먼트에서 경쟁해요 .

D Rearrange and write the sentences.

❶ 우리는 매일 운동해요.
every day / exercise / We / .
We exercise every day.

❷ 축구는 우리가 가장 좋아하는 스포츠예요.
Soccer / our / is / sport / favorite / .
Soccer is our favorite sport.

100 101

Day 15

P103

Pop Quiz ☑ 길 ☐ 안개 ☐ 위험 ☑ 사고

P106~107

Skill UP

A Choose and write the words.

fog scare bicycle

❶ bicycle 자전거
❷ fog 안개
❸ scare 겁주다, 겁먹다

B Cross out, unscramble, and write the words.

❶ 피하다 a~~m~~ivod — avoid
❷ 사고 cad~~x~~ntice — accident
❸ 위험 d~~b~~gnare — danger
❹ 예방하다, 막다 evp~~d~~rnet — prevent

C Unscramble and complete the sentences.

❶ 도로에 많은 차들이 있어요. ardo
There are many cars on the road.

❷ 그는 교통사고를 당했어요. aicdcent
He had a car accident.

❸ 그 표지판은 위험을 나타내요. dgnare
The sign says danger.

D Choose and complete the sentences.

bicycle fog avoid

❶ 안개가 짙어요.
The fog is thick.

❷ 나는 자전거를 타요.
I ride my bicycle.

❸ 우리는 위험을 피해야 해요.
We should avoid danger.

Day 11~15

P108

WORD PUZZLE Complete the word puzzle.

P110

Review TEST 맞힌 개수 : /40

❶ tell	이야기를 하다, 말하다	㉑ 배경	background
❷ picture	그림, 사진	㉒ 무대, 단계	stage
❸ fantastic	환상적인	㉓ 노래	song
❹ superb	대단히 훌륭한, 최고의	㉔ 천재, 천재성	genius
❺ cheap	(값이) 싼	㉕ 판매	sale
❻ expensive	비싼	㉖ 할인한 물건, 흥정	bargain
❼ pay	지불하다, 내다	㉗ 서둘러 가다, 돌진	dash
❽ coin	동전	㉘ 외상, 신용 거래	credit
❾ father	아버지	㉙ 생일	birthday
❿ mother	어머니	㉚ 전통	tradition
⓫ parents	부모님	㉛ 기념일	anniversary
⓬ surprise	놀라움, 깜짝 놀라게 하기	㉜ 친구	friend
⓭ baseball	야구	㉝ 운동하다, 운동	exercise
⓮ basketball	농구	㉞ 운동선수	athlete
⓯ defeat	이기다, (상대를) 패배시키다	㉟ 경쟁하다, 겨루다	compete
⓰ condition	(경기자의) 컨디션, 상태, 조건	㊱ 축구	soccer
⓱ road	도로, 길	㊲ 사고	accident
⓲ bicycle	자전거	㊳ 예방하다, 막다	prevent
⓳ danger	위험	㊴ 겁주다, 겁먹다	scare
⓴ fog	안개	㊵ 피하다	avoid

Day 16

P113

Pop Quiz ☑ 공주 ☐ 왕자 ☐ 왕 ☑ 여왕

P116~117

Skill Up

A Find, circle, and write the words.

❶ 왕	yuw(king)z	king	
❷ 왕자	js(prince)	prince	
❸ 성	bk(castle)	castle	
❹ 여왕	lf(queen)g	queen	

B Choose and write the words.

princess coast locate treasure

❶	공주	princess	princess
❷	해안	coast	coast
❸	보물	treasure	treasure
❹	(특정 위치에) 두다	locate	locate

116

C Connect and fill in the blanks.

❶ The princess looks pretty.
공주 는 예뻐 보여요.

❷ The place is near the coast.
그 장소는 해안 근처에 있어요.

❸ The treasure is in the castle.
그 보물 은 성 안에 있어요.

D Rearrange and write the sentences.

❶ 그들은 성에 살아요.
in / live / They / a castle / .
They live in a castle.

❷ 왕은 경비병을 배치할 거예요.
locate / The king / will / his guards / .
The king will locate his guards.

117

Day 17

P119

Pop Quiz ☑ 무리, 집단 ☐ 소리, 소음 ☑ 문제 ☐ 나이

P122~123

Skill Up

A Choose and write the words.

guy disturb group

❶ group	❷ guy	❸ disturb
그룹, 무리, 집단	남자, 사람	방해하다

B Cross out, unscramble, and write the words.

❶ 소리, 소음	n x i s o e	noise
❷ 실수, 잘못, 오해하다	t a m g s i e k	mistake
❸ 견디다, 참다	u e n g d r e	endure
❹ 문제	p r b d e m l o	problem

122

C Unscramble and complete the sentences.

❶ 내 나이는 10살이에요. e g a
My age is ten.

❷ 사이렌은 큰 소리를 내요. o i s n e
A siren makes a loud noise .

❸ 나는 더위를 견딜 수 없어요. d e n r e u
I can't endure the heat.

D Choose and complete the sentences.

mistake problem group

❶ 나는 스터디 그룹을 만들었어요.
I made a study group .

❷ 나는 큰 실수를 했어요.
I made a big mistake .

❸ 나는 이 문제를 해결할 수 없어요.
I can't solve this problem .

123

Day 18

P125

Pop Quiz ☑ 손목시계 ☐ 안경 ☑ 신발 ☐ 가죽

P128~129

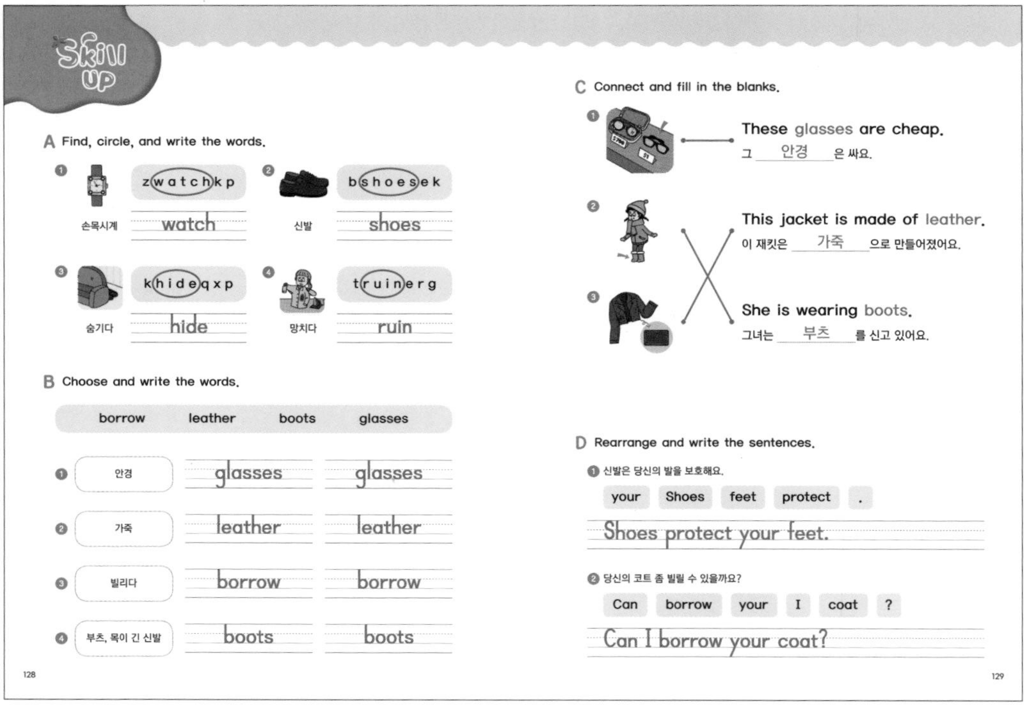

Skill up

A Find, circle, and write the words.

1 zwatchkp — watch (손목시계)
2 bshoesek — shoes (신발)
3 khideqxp — hide (숨기다)
4 truinerg — ruin (망치다)

B Choose and write the words.

borrow leather boots glasses

1 안경 glasses glasses
2 가죽 leather leather
3 빌리다 borrow borrow
4 부츠, 목이 긴 신발 boots boots

128

C Connect and fill in the blanks.

1 These glasses are cheap.
그 안경 은 싸요.

2 This jacket is made of leather.
이 재킷은 가죽 으로 만들어졌어요.

3 She is wearing boots.
그녀는 부츠 를 신고 있어요.

D Rearrange and write the sentences.

1 신발은 당신의 발을 보호해요.
your Shoes feet protect .
Shoes protect your feet.

2 당신의 코트 좀 빌릴 수 있을까요?
Can borrow your I coat ?
Can I borrow your coat?

129

Day 19

P131

Pop Quiz ☐ 설탕 ☑ 소금 ☑ 맛있는 ☐ 두꺼운

P134~135

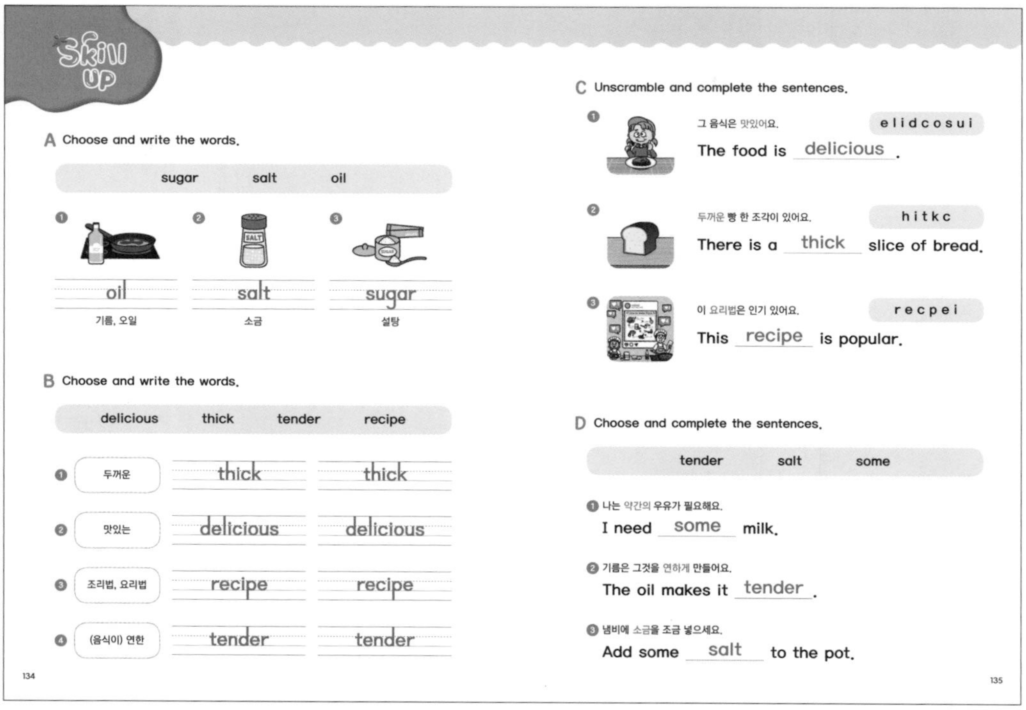

Skill up

A Choose and write the words.

sugar salt oil

1 oil (기름, 오일)
2 salt (소금)
3 sugar (설탕)

B Choose and write the words.

delicious thick tender recipe

1 두꺼운 thick thick
2 맛있는 delicious delicious
3 조리법, 요리법 recipe recipe
4 (음식이) 연한 tender tender

134

C Unscramble and complete the sentences.

1 그 음식은 맛있어요. elidcosui
The food is delicious .

2 두꺼운 빵 한 조각이 있어요. hitkc
There is a thick slice of bread.

3 이 요리법은 인기 있어요. recpei
This recipe is popular.

D Choose and complete the sentences.

tender salt some

1 나는 약간의 우유가 필요해요.
I need some milk.

2 기름은 그것을 연하게 만들어요.
The oil makes it tender .

3 냄비에 소금을 조금 넣으세요.
Add some salt to the pot.

135

Day 20

P137

Pop Quiz ☐ 부엌 ☑ 거실 ☑ 침실 ☐ 욕실

P140~141

Skill up

A Choose and write the words.

garden bedroom bathroom

1. bedroom 침실
2. garden 정원
3. bathroom 욕실, 화장실

B Cross out, unscramble, and write the words.

1. 부엌 c k i h t n ~~a~~ e — kitchen
2. 관찰하다 o v b e s r e ~~p~~ — observe
3. 완벽한, 이상적인 ~~b~~ e i d l a — ideal
4. 장점 e m r ~~x~~ t i — merit

C Connect and fill in the blanks.

1. My dad is in the living room. 우리 아빠는 거실 에 계세요.
2. My mom is in the kitchen. 우리 엄마는 부엌 에 계세요.
3. I observe the moon with a telescope. 나는 망원경으로 달을 관찰해요 .

D Rearrange and write the sentences.

1. 우리 할머니는 정원에 계세요.
My / the garden / is / grandma / in / .
My grandma is in the garden.

2. 내 남동생은 욕실에 있어요.
the bathroom / brother / My / is / in / .
My brother is in the bathroom.

140 141

Day 16~20

P142

WORD SEARCH

Find and circle the hidden pictures. Then write the words.

leather, treasure, watch, glasses, shoes, salt, oil, sugar

142

P144

Review TEST

맞힌 개수 : ☐ /40

1 king	왕	21 성	castle
2 queen	여왕	22 보물	treasure
3 prince	왕자	23 해안	coast
4 locate	(특정 위치에) 두다	24 공주	princess
5 age	나이	25 남자, 사람	guy
6 mistake	실수, 잘못, 오해하다	26 문제	problem
7 group	그룹, 무리, 집단	27 방해하다	disturb
8 noise	소리, 소음	28 견디다, 참다	endure
9 watch	손목시계	29 빌리다	borrow
10 glasses	안경	30 망치다	ruin
11 boots	부츠, 목이 긴 신발	31 숨기다	hide
12 shoes	신발	32 가죽	leather
13 salt	소금	33 약간의, 조금	some
14 sugar	설탕	34 (음식이) 연한	tender
15 oil	기름, 오일	35 조리법, 요리법	recipe
16 delicious	맛있는	36 두꺼운	thick
17 bathroom	욕실, 화장실	37 정원	garden
18 ideal	완벽한, 이상적인	38 침실	bedroom
19 kitchen	부엌	39 관찰하다	observe
20 living room	거실	40 장점	merit

144

Day 21

P147

Pop Quiz ☐ 호수 ☑ 방학 ☑ 모래 ☐ 잔디

P150~151

Skill Up

A Find, circle, and write the words.

1. 돌 — y(stone)wg — stone
2. 언덕 — ps(hill)ek — hill
3. 모래 — uwoh(sand) — sand
4. 호수 — q(lake)mrt — lake

B Choose and write the words.

exhausted remote vacation grass

1. 외딴, 먼 — remote — remote
2. 방학, 휴가 — vacation — vacation
3. 잔디 — grass — grass
4. 기진맥진한 — exhausted — exhausted

150

C Unscramble and complete the sentences.

1. covaanit
나는 방학 동안 캠핑을 하러 갔어요.
I went camping during the vacation.
2. mereto
이 외딴 곳은 조용해요.
This remote place is calm.
3. ssagr
우리는 잔디 위에 누워요.
We lie on the grass.

D Choose and complete the sentences.

hill lake sand

1. 그들은 모래에서 놀아요.
They play in the sand.
2. 오리 몇 마리가 호수에 있어요.
Some ducks are on the lake.
3. 그가 언덕에 올라요.
He climbs the hill.

151

Day 22

P153

Pop Quiz ☑ 필요하다 ☐ 선택하다 ☑ 운 좋은 ☐ 전달하다

P156~157

Skill Up

A Choose and write the words.

emotion miss carry

1. carry — 전달하다, 나르다
2. miss — 그리워하다, 놓치다
3. emotion — 감정

B Choose and write the words.

choose environment need understand

1. 이해하다 — understand — understand
2. 환경 — environment — environment
3. 선택하다 — choose — choose
4. 필요하다 — need — need

156

C Connect and fill in the blanks.

1. I'm fortunate to have a big family.
나는 대가족이라 운이 좋아 요.
2. I can understand.
나는 이해할 수 있어요.
3. I choose words carefully.
나는 단어를 신중하게 선택해요.

D Rearrange and write the sentences.

1. 나는 당신의 감정들을 느낄 수 있어요.
I / feel / can / emotions / your / .
I can feel your emotions.
2. 나는 내 친구가 그리워요.
my / friend / miss / I / .
I miss my friend.

157

Day 23

P159

Pop Quiz ☐ 돌보다 ☑ 울다 ☑ 매달리다 ☐ 이해하다

P162~163

Skill Up

A Find, circle, and write the words.

1. 아이, 어린이 — s(child)wy — child
2. 어른, 성인 — sh(adult)k — adult
3. 탄생, 출생 — u(birth)qpd — birth
4. 괴물 — n(monster) — monster

B Cross out, unscramble, and write the words.

1. 돌보다, 돌봄, 보살핌 — r m̶ c e a — care
2. 울다 — c k̶ y r — cry
3. 매달리다, 달라붙다 — c i g x̶ l n — cling
4. 아기, 유아 — f a x̶ n t i n — infant

C Connect and fill in the blanks.

1. The children cling to their mother.
아이들이 엄마에게 매달려요.
2. The infant slept soundly.
그 아기는 푹 잤어요.
3. Does she cry in the night?
그녀가 밤중에 우나요?

D Choose and complete the sentences.

cares birth child

1. 그녀는 아픈 자녀들을 돌봐요.
She cares for her sick children.
2. 한 아이가 책을 읽고 있어요.
A child is reading a book.
3. 우리는 내 아기의 탄생을 축하했어요.
We celebrated the birth of my baby.

162 163

Day 24

P165

Pop Quiz ☑ 속상한 ☐ 게으른 ☑ 수줍어하는 ☐ 사회적인

P168~169

Skill Up

A Choose and write the words.

shy glad crazy

1. glad — 기쁜
2. crazy — 정상이 아닌, 미친
3. shy — 수줍어하는

B Cross out, unscramble, and write the words.

1. 안정된, 차분한 — t e s a l b x̶ — stable
2. 화난, 속상한 — u x̶ p e t s — upset
3. 사교적인, 사회적인 — x̶ c i s a l o — social
4. 재치, 기지 — w x̶ i t — wit

C Unscramble and complete the sentences.

1. 그녀는 게으르다고 느꼈어요. (z l a y)
She was feeling lazy.
2. 그녀는 화가 났어요. (e u p s t)
She is upset.
3. 그녀는 재치를 뽐냈어요. (t i w)
She showed off her wit.

D Rearrange and write the sentences.

1. 나는 당신을 만나서 기뻐요.
I glad you am to see .
I am glad to see you.
2. 그 여자아이는 수줍어해요.
is The girl shy .
The girl is shy.

168 169

Day 25

P171

Pop Quiz ☐ 남편 ☑ 아내 ☐ 주요한 ☑ 함께

P174~175

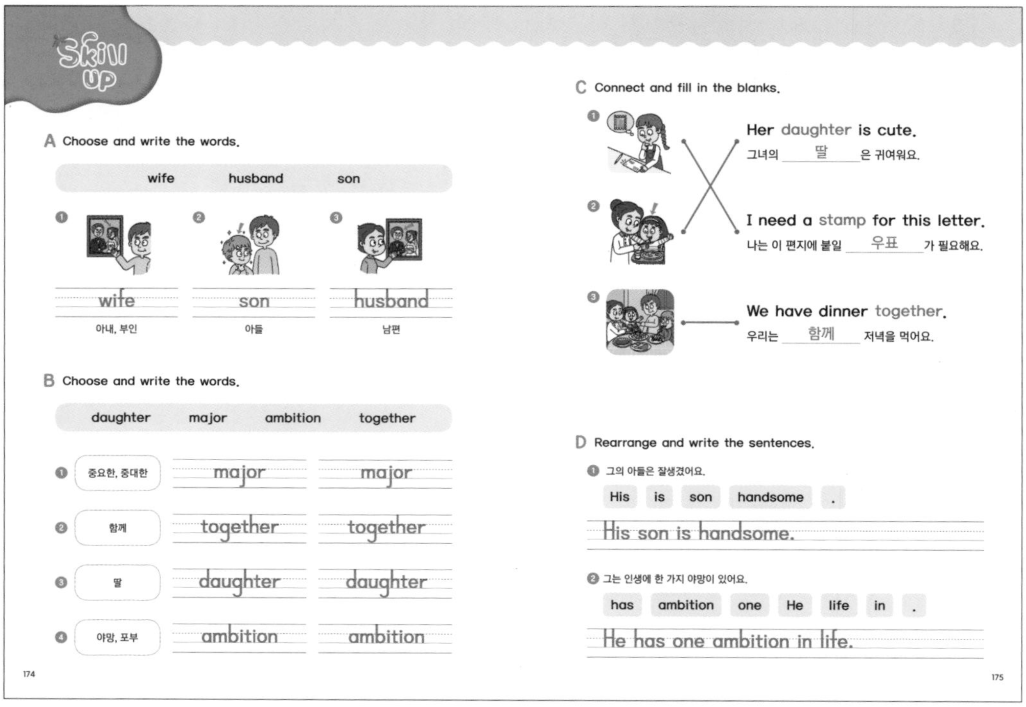

Skill up

A Choose and write the words.

wife husband son

1. wife (아내, 부인)
2. son (아들)
3. husband (남편)

B Choose and write the words.

daughter major ambition together

1. 중요한, 중대한 — major major
2. 함께 — together together
3. 딸 — daughter daughter
4. 야망, 포부 — ambition ambition

C Connect and fill in the blanks.

1. Her daughter is cute. 그녀의 딸 은 귀여워요.
2. I need a stamp for this letter. 나는 이 편지에 붙일 우표 가 필요해요.
3. We have dinner together. 우리는 함께 저녁을 먹어요.

D Rearrange and write the sentences.

1. 그의 아들은 잘생겼어요.
His / is / son / handsome / .
His son is handsome.
2. 그는 인생에 한 가지 야망이 있어요.
has / ambition / one / He / life / in / .
He has one ambition in life.

174 175

Day 20~25

P176

WORD PUZZLE Complete the word puzzle.

ACROSS: 2 shy, 3 adult, 5 carry, 7 miss, 8 stone

DOWN: 1 crazy, 2 stamp, 4 grass, 5 child, 6 wife

ACROSS
② The girl is ______.
③ He is an ______.
⑤ They ______ a message for the king.
⑦ I ______ my friend.
⑧ I collect ______s.

DOWN
① He is ______.
② I need a ______ for this letter.
④ We lie on the ______.
⑤ A ______ is reading a book.
⑥ She is my ______.

176

P178

Review TEST 맞힌 개수 : /40

1 grass	잔디	21 호수	lake
2 stone	돌	22 방학, 휴가	vacation
3 sand	모래	23 기진맥진한	exhausted
4 hill	언덕	24 외딴, 먼	remote
5 miss	그리워하다, 놓치다	25 이해하다	understand
6 need	필요하다	26 운 좋은	fortunate
7 choose	선택하다	27 환경	environment
8 carry	전달하다, 나르다	28 감정	emotion
9 child	아이, 어린이	29 울다	cry
10 adult	어른, 성인	30 아기, 유아	infant
11 care	돌보다, 돌봄, 보살핌	31 탄생, 출생	birth
12 cling	매달리다, 달라붙다	32 괴물	monster
13 glad	기쁜	33 수줍어하는	shy
14 upset	화난, 속상한	34 안정된, 차분한	stable
15 crazy	정상이 아닌, 미친	35 재치, 기지	wit
16 social	사교적인, 사회적인	36 게으른	lazy
17 husband	남편	37 함께	together
18 wife	아내, 부인	38 중요한, 중대한	major
19 daughter	딸	39 우표, 도장	stamp
20 son	아들	40 야망, 포부	ambition

178

Word List

a

accident	사고
actual	실제의
adult	어른, 성인
advise	충고하다
age	나이
allow	허락하다
ambition	야망, 포부
animal	동물
anniversary	기념일
answer	대답하다
art	미술
ask	묻다
athlete	운동선수
atmosphere	분위기, 대기
avoid	피하다

b

back	허리, 등
background	배경
bake	굽다
bargain	할인한 물건, 흥정
baseball	야구
basketball	농구
bathroom	욕실, 화장실
bear	곰
beautiful	아름다운
bedroom	침실
bicycle	자전거
birth	탄생, 출생
birthday	생일
bitter	맛이 쓴, 격렬한
boots	부츠, 목이 긴 신발
boring	따분한, 지루한
borrow	빌리다
brilliant	뛰어난, 훌륭한

c

calm	침착한, 차분한
care	돌보다, 돌봄, 보살핌
carry	전달하다, 나르다
castle	성
cheap	(값이) 싼
child	아이, 어린이
chill	냉기, 오한
chin	턱
choose	선택하다
clever	영리한
climate	기후
cling	매달리다, 달라붙다
coast	해안
coin	동전
compete	경쟁하다, 겨루다
condition	(경기자의) 컨디션, 상태, 조건
crazy	정상이 아닌, 미친
credit	외상, 신용 거래
cry	울다

d

danger	위험
dash	서둘러 가다, 돌진
daughter	딸
defeat	이기다, (상대를) 패배시키다
delicious	맛있는
disturb	방해하다
door	문
drug	약

e

elegant	우아한
elephant	코끼리
emotion	감정
endure	견디다, 참다
entire	전체의, 온
environment	환경
escape	달아나다, 탈출하다
examine	진찰하다, 조사하다
exercise	운동하다, 운동
exhausted	기진맥진한
expensive	비싼
experience	경험
expert	전문가

f

fall	가을
fantastic	환상적인
fat	뚱뚱한
father	아버지
favorite	매우 좋아하는
feel	느끼다
finger	손가락
floor	바닥, 층
fog	안개
fortunate	운 좋은
friend	친구
full	배부른

g

garden	정원
genius	천재, 천재성
get	받다, 구하다
give	주다
glad	기쁜
glasses	안경
grass	잔디
group	그룹, 무리, 집단
guy	남자, 사람

h

hide	숨기다
hill	언덕
hole	구멍
hospital	병원
hungry	배고픈
husband	남편

i

ideal	완벽한, 이상적인
infant	아기, 유아
invite	초대하다

k

king	왕
kitchen	부엌
knee	무릎
knock	노크하다, 두드리다

l

lake	호수

lazy	게으른
leather	가죽
listen	듣다
living room	거실
locate	(특정 위치에) 두다
love	사랑하다
loyal	충성스러운

m

major	중요한, 중대한
math	수학
merit	장점
mild	온화한, 순한
miss	그리워하다, 놓치다
mistake	실수, 잘못, 오해하다
monkey	원숭이
monster	괴물
mother	어머니
music	음악

n

need	필요하다
noise	소리, 소음

o

observe	관찰하다
oil	기름, 오일

p

parents	부모님
passage	통로, 복도
patient	인내심 있는, 환자
pay	지불하다, 내다
picture	그림, 사진
precious	소중한, 귀중한
prevent	예방하다, 막다
prince	왕자
princess	공주
problem	문제

q

queen	여왕

r

recipe	조리법, 요리법
remember	기억하다
remote	외딴, 먼
road	도로, 길
ruin	망치다

s

sale	판매
salt	소금
sand	모래
scare	겁주다, 겁먹다
science	과학
seal	밀봉하다
season	계절
send	보내다
shoes	신발
shy	수줍어하는
skill	기술, 기량
smart	똑똑한
soccer	축구
social	사교적인, 사회적인
solve	풀다, 해결하다
some	약간의, 조금
son	아들
song	노래
speak	말하다
spring	봄
stable	안정된, 차분한
stage	무대, 단계
stairs	계단
stamp	우표, 도장
stone	돌
strong	강한
subject	과목, 주제
sugar	설탕
summer	여름
superb	대단히 훌륭한, 최고의
surprise	놀라움, 깜짝 놀라게 하기
sweet	달콤한

t

talent	재능, 재주
tea	차, 찻잎
tell	이야기를 하다, 말하다
tender	(음식이) 연한
thick	두꺼운
toe	발가락
together	함께
trace	추적하다, 흔적
tradition	전통
treasure	보물

u

ugly	못생긴
understand	이해하다
upset	화난, 속상한

v

vacation	방학, 휴가

w

wall	벽
watch	손목시계
weak	약한
wife	아내, 부인
window	창문
winter	겨울
wit	재치, 기지
wonder	궁금해하다

z

zebra	얼룩말